SPIRITUAL DETOXIFICATION AND SOULS RENEWAL

HEALTHY CHURCH
BIBLE STUDY SERIES

Volume Three

Copyright © 2021 by **Adebayo S. David**

Paperbook ISBN: 978-1-952098-60-4

Printed in the United States of America. All rights reserved solely by the publisher. This book or parts thereof may not be reproduced in any form, stored in a retrieval system, or transmitted in any form by any means - electronic, mechanical, photocopy. Unless otherwise noted, Bible quotations are taken from the Holy Bible, New King James Version (NKJV) Copyright 1982 by Thomas Nelson, Inc., publishers. Used by permission.

Cornerstone Publishing

A Division of Cornerstone Creativity Group LLC
Phone: +1(516) 547-4999
info@thecornerstonepublishers.com
www.thecornerstonepublishers.com

To order bulk copies of this book or to contact the author please email: greaterthingsnow@yahoo.com

INTRODUCTION

The HEALTHY CHURCH SERIES is a series of Bible study teachings developed to encourage pastors to build a healthy church environment, based on the word of God, where believers can grow, learn and thrive spiritually, mentally, maritally and financially in life and in the kingdom of God. This is in with Paul's admonition in

1 Timothy 3:15 to teach people how to behave in the house of God, which is the church of the living God, "THE PILLAR AND GROUND OF TRUTH".

This book is designed to ensure godly characters and attitudes in believers that can make them succeed anywhere and in all aspects of life – personal Christian walk, marriage, ministry, business, academics and relationships of any kind - knowing full well the word of God and the mind of God concerning any subject that affects their lives in Christ.

Nations and people that prosper are people who have built their lives on the "truth of life" - which is Jesus Christ. He said, "You shall know the truth and the truth shall set you free. Only the truth that you know and the truth that is revealed to you can set you free!

CONTENTS

STUDY 1

NECESSITY OF SPIRITUAL DETOXIFICATION

Text: 2 Peter 1:8-9

> *"For if these things be in you, and abound, they make you that ye shall neither be barren nor unfruitful in the knowledge of our Lord Jesus Christ. But he that lacketh these things is blind, and cannot see afar off, and hath forgotten that he was purged from his old sins."*

Detoxification is often used in medicine and healthcare to refer to the process of neutralizing or eliminating toxins from the body. Toxins are poisonous substances produced within living organisms, including human beings. They come from different sources, including the food we eat and our environment. If left to accumulate, toxins can cause a disruption in the flow of fresh life in a living organism, as well as posing serious health risks to the body.

So also is the life of a Christian. We are spiritual living organisms and living stones, built by God to produce His fresh life in us and through us to our communities, the church of God and the society, in general. 1 Peter 2:5-7 affirms this: "Ye also, as lively stones, are built up a spiritual house, a holy priesthood, to offer up spiritual sacrifices, acceptable to God by Jesus Christ. Wherefore also it is contained in the scripture, Behold, I lay in Sion a chief cornerstone, elect, precious: and he that believeth on him shall not be confounded. Unto you therefore which believe He is precious: but unto them which be disobedient, the stone which the builders disallowed, the same is made the head of the corner."

Thus, as living stones in the house of God and living new creatures in Christ Jesus, we must feed our new life with the right food, so that we can have a healthy growth. We must repel and reject anything that may constitute a toxin in our lives or that may disrupt the flow of the life of God in us and through us.

FEED HEALTHY, GROW HEALTHY

Most of the toxins in the human body come from foods – foods that are unhealthy or have been genetically modified (GMO). There are many genetically modified spiritual foods that are being presented in churches. These foods taste good and feel great, but they have death in them. Detoxification, therefore, begins with watching what we eat and eating the right foods. 1 Peter 2:2 says, "As newborn babes, desire the sincere milk of the word that ye may grow thereby."

Healthy diets serve the triple functions of preventing toxins from entering our body, cleansing traces of toxins from our body, and ensuring that our body has a healthy growth. Similarly, growing up spiritually requires good food and nourishment to make the life of God flow freely in us, around us and through us. Therefore, we must be mindful of what we feed on spiritually. There are all kinds of foods that baby Christians would like to feed on. Like growing kids, they want all kinds of sweet things but some sweet things may be dangerous to health. Here, for example, is what Dr. Robert F. DeMaria says about sugar, in his book, A HEALTHIER YOU:

"Sugar handcuffs your white blood cells from performing their job. A can of soda with nine and a half spoons of sugar depresses your immune system by up to 25 percent for five to six hours. People who eat sugar are always sick and never 100 percent healthy. Stevia, honey, maple syrups are alternatives to sugar."

Therefore, as believers, we cannot just feed on spiritual junk foods because they taste good or feel good. Neither can we hold on to our ungodly or unhealthy behaviors because they make us feel good or feel like champions, especially when they are contrary to the word of God.

THE DIET OF CONQUERORS

Hebrews 5:14 reveals: "But strong meat belongeth to them that are of full age, even those who by reason of use have their senses exercised to discern both good and evil."

To grow up into healthier, stronger, well-developed and truly mature believers in Christ Jesus, it is important that we eat the right food. This is the only way we can withstand the wiles of Satan and fulfil our mandates on earth. Strong meat or healthy food is for serious-minded Christians. Any food that is not spiritually healthy for us produces toxins that will choke the life of God in us. The life of God requires the right spiritual diets of biblical principles and Christ-like living. You must avoid things that choke the life of God. Things that choke the life of God in a Christian are things that defile, corrupt and make us spiritually sick, inactive, and unable to walk and work triumphantly with Him.

Hebrews 12:15-17 warns: "Looking diligently lest any man fail of the grace of God; lest any root of bitterness springing up trouble you, and thereby many be defiled; Lest there be any fornicator, or profane person, as Esau, who for one morsel of meat sold his birthright. For ye know how that afterward, when he would have inherited the blessing, he was rejected: for he found no place of repentance, though he sought it carefully with tears."

The above verses reveal some spiritual toxins that we must avoid in our Christian life. It specifically mentions the roots of bitterness that can spring up within us and cause defilement for us and for others. These roots of bitterness are not only orchestrated to defile us but to choke God's very life and power from our lives.

Spiritual toxins generally give us a chokehold, such that we are not able to breathe well spiritually. Indeed, their ultimate goal is to stop us from breathing altogether. And when we can no longer breathe, it means we are dead. Sadly, many believers are living dead. The toxins of life have choked God's life from within them and they are not able to breathe the fresh life of God. Consequently, they can no longer enjoy the things of God or even life as a whole. They find it hard to enjoy their family or prosper in their endeavors. Worse still, they can no longer run their heavenly race. This is why we must do all we can to avoid spiritual toxins, no matter how appealing they may seem to us.

We must be careful with the things we put in our spirit man, lest we are defiled and corrupted. Whatever goes into a man becomes the man. Whatever you are hearing and feeding on becomes you. Jesus said, "Take heed what ye hear" (Mark 4: 24). In other words, be careful what you allow into your spirit and heart; it might become life or death to you – that is, a toxin or an antioxidant (toxin-killer).

PRAYERS

1. My Father, detoxify me of every wrong food that I have eaten that has corrupted my soul.

2. O Lord, deliver me from every wrong soul-tie of the spirit and flesh.
3. Whatever that has defiled me, knowingly or unknowingly, I cleanse myself with the blood of Jesus.

STUDY 2

RECOGNIZING SPIRITUAL TOXINS

Text: 2 Kings 4:39-41

> *"And one went out into the field to gather herbs, and found a wild vine, and gathered thereof wild gourds his lap full, and came and shred them into the pot of pottage: for they knew them not. So they poured out for the men to eat. And it came to pass, as they were eating of the pottage, that they cried out, and said, O thou man of God, there is death in the pot. And they could not eat thereof. But he said, Then bring meal. And he cast it into the pot; and he said, Pour out for the people, that they may eat. And there was no harm in the pot."*

Much of the so-called spiritual food that is served in many churches today and consumed by many Christians is nothing but death in the pot. Such food includes teachings that do not lead to transformation of souls, purification of character, or preparation for eternity. Most of these teachings only focus on breakthrough, prosperity and success; but of what use are these things, if we end up losing our souls?

Christ has clearly warned, "Take heed and beware of covetousness, for a man's life consisteth not in the abundance of the things which he possesseth." (Luke 12:15). Yet, all that many churches teach their congregations daily and what many believers pray about is how to pursue and have increasing abundance. This kind of food does not save our souls; nor does it correct us, chastise our flesh, or point us to eternity. It is all about this present world.

This brings us back to the story of Elisha and the sons of the prophets in our text. It happened that as they were cooking and making mass food for all to eat, one of the sons of the prophets saw wild gourds and he thought it was a good recipe to be added to the meal. But as soon as the meal was done and the eating began, they felt a sharp poison in the meal and shouted to the prophet, "O thou man of God, there is death in the pot."

There is a lot of death being served in our churches today, but the poisons are being sugarcoated or disguised by crafty pastors and church-leaders. This is similar to what the American company, Senomyx, is doing today, with the claim that it has "reverse engineered" human taste and aroma receptors. The company has developed special chemicals (flavor enhancers) that mask bitter flavors in food and beverages by turning off bitter flavor receptors on the tongue and enhancing the sweet and salty. So, even if the original ingredient of a food product is bitter, it can begin to taste sweet to the consumer with the addition of these chemicals.

In the same way, many sermons today are packaged and flavored to taste and feel good, but they are actually transferring spiritual toxins and death to those consuming them. The preachers of such sermons are those the Scripture aptly describes as having "impressive credentials and bewitching performances" Matthew 24: 23-25, MSG). We must be vigilant, so as not be ensnared by such preachers and their enticing words.

Let's take a deeper look at attitudes, habits, pursuits, and lifestyles that constitute "death in the pot" or choking toxins to our spiritual life.

TYPES OF SPIRITUAL TOXINS

1. Worries and cares.

Isn't it incredible that since mankind has been worrying, fretting and getting anxious about their issues, none of these engagements has ever solved their problems? When you worry about money, for example, the worry never puts cash in your pocket; and your situation remains the same, until you go and work for money or pray by faith and believe God for your needs.

Jesus said, "Therefore I say unto you, Take no thought for your life, what ye shall eat, or what ye shall drink..."

(Matthew 6:25). Why? Because worry has never produced anything good, except discouragement, depression, fear, frustration, heart attacks, hypertension, strokes, paralysis, and, of course, PRAYERLESSNESS. The saying indeed is true – "A worrying Christian is a prayerless Christian; and a praying Christian is a 'worry-less' Christian."

The fact that worry and cares are toxins that have the power to choke our spiritual life is emphasized in Mark 4:19, "And the cares of this world, and the deceitfulness of riches, and the lusts of other things entering in, choke the word, and it becometh unfruitful."

2. Unforgiveness and malice.

Unforgiveness and malice are spiritual toxins that choke believers spiritually. They develop in you a gall that makes you bitter towards others, yourself, and God. Moreover, they can drive away potential helpers and also destroy opportunities that are meant to lead to breakthroughs and promotion .

However, the greatest danger that unforgiveness and malice pose to our spiritual life is what Jesus revealed in Matthew 6:15, "But if ye forgive not men their trespasses, neither will your Father forgive your trespasses." So, beloved, are you sure you have really forgiven that offense against you? Those injuries and betrayal – have you forgiven them?

I know it is sometimes hard to forgive, but the fire of

eternal judgment is fiercer than the pain of any offense or hurt. You just have to let it go. That betrayal from a friend, spouse, parent, child, boss, or an associate that abandoned you when you needed them the most can hurt so badly. But when you think of the fire of hell and eternal damnation, you would understand that it is better to suffer the pain of betrayals and forgive and enjoy eternal bliss with God. May the Lord help us and cure us of the toxins that seek to hinder our everlasting joy.

3. Bitterness, anger and rage

The combination of bitterness, anger and rage usually feels like a good meal for our carnal mind. It feels good when we get even, or try to carry out our threats; but in the end, it destroys us. On September 11, 2020, a pastor shot his wife dead in Florida, Unites States. The question is, what could have warranted such a deadly attack? Anger, rage, bitterness and other similar factors that we cannot fathom. This shows that when we don't detoxify ourselves of these evils, they eventually destroy us. This is why Ephesians 4:31 exhorts, "Let all bitterness and wrath and anger and clamor and evil speaking be put away from you, with all malice."

A preacher once said, "Whenever there is an issue in marriage, the stronger one should be the first to forgive and let go." Beloved, sometimes it is easier said than done, but the truth is, if we must make eternity, we need to forgive and get rid of this toxin that wants to send us to hell-fire. Anger, bitterness and rage seem sweet when we hold on to them or engage in them, but they eventually destroy us, our testimony and faith. No wonder the Scripture says "...Be not hasty in thy spirit to be angry: for anger resteth in the bosom of fools" (Ecclesiastes 7:9). Don't be a fool! DETOXIFY.

4. Fornication and sexual immorality

Beloved, sexual sins are very pleasurable, especially when you do not know God or you are a struggling Christian. Sex without commitment seems sweet. It seems exciting, but it destroys one's soul in the end. The Scripture says, "Stolen waters are sweet, and bread eaten in secret is pleasant. But he knoweth not that the dead are there; and that her guests are in the depths of hell" (Proverbs 9:17-18).

When we engage in any kind of sexual immorality, such as fornication, adultery, masturbation, pornography, incest, homosexuality, lesbianism or bestiality, the danger to our souls is enormous. It kills us spiritually, mentally, emotionally and psychologically. It robs us of our confidence and boldness in Christ. You cannot commit fornication, adultery or masturbation and feel confident to approach the throne of God or confront demons. You will quake at the presence of demons.

Sexual sins have more weight than any other sins a man commits. The Scripture warns, "Flee fornication. Every sin that a man doeth is without the body; but he that committeth fornication sinneth against his own body." (1 Corinthians 6:18).

Consequences of sexual sins include:

- It stains your spiritual garment and makes the land vomit you (Leviticus 18:22-26).
- It makes you lose confidence and boldness (Proverbs 28:1).
- You can contact STDs (Deuteronomy 28:27).
- It brings shame and dishonor (Proverbs 6:33).
- You are partially possessed or obsessed (2 Samuel 13:2).
- You will suffer from partial madness. You will misbehave when you see some members of the opposite gender (Ecclesiastes 10 :12-13).
- You are like a city broken down without walls. Spiritual jackals, cockroaches and rodents will invade your life (Proverbs 25:28).
- You lose your mental capabilities. Gradually, your ability to retain and memorize scriptures and other important information will begin to disappear. In other words, you suffer partial amnesia (Proverbs 7:1-7).

- You lose self-confidence in the assembly of the saints (Proverbs 6:32-33).
- It steals your money and your substance is in the house of the harlot. Your cars, buildings, ministry, dignity and future are mortgaged for momentary pleasures (Proverbs 29:3).
- It causes death and destruction (Proverbs 2:18; 7:27).
- You are reduced to a piece of bread (Proverbs 6:26).
- With pornography, you suffer from multiple personality disorder and bipolar disorder. Pornography makes you one with those numerous men and women you watch. Whatever spirit that is in those individuals, a little here and there of them, is deposited in you and controls your life. 1 Corinthians 6:16 says, "…He which is joined to an harlot is one body."
- It brings divine judgment on earth and in eternity. "Marriage is honourable in all, and the bed undefiled: but whoremongers and adulterers God will judge." (Hebrews 13:4).

Specifically for pornography, if you desire true freedom, you must detoxify yourself of the spirits and multiple personalities that are in you. Prayers of deliverance and regular association with godly brethren with a passion for holiness will help. Destroy tapes, videos, images, and books that stimulate your sensual and sexual appetite. Block pornographic websites and avoid sexual innuendoes and suggestions to your soul.

This is a real battle and you must not stop praying and fighting until you win. Even if you find yourself doing it or going back to it, keep praying, keep fighting, keep seeking freedom. I guarantee you that, suddenly, the desires will disappear. Above all, be accountable to mature believers, who can help you in prayers and protect you - not those who will gossip about you or use you as a sermon note or threaten to implicate you.

5. Strange doctrines and inability to endure sound doctrines

With regard to the present time, 2 Timothy 4:3 has rightly predicted: "For the time will come when they will not endure sound doctrine; but after their own lusts shall they heap to themselves teachers, having itching ears."

Strange doctrines are sweet, enticing and inviting but they are also very destructive. Such doctrines intoxicate us with deceptions and delusions that are meant to lure our souls to destruction. Examples of the messages of such doctrines include: "No hell, heaven is for all"; "Once saved, forever saved"; "You can masturbate or commit adultery, God understands"; "You can divorce multiple times, God understands", and so on.

Many of such teachings are sweet to those with itching ears; but they are toxins that will destroy our souls.

6. Love of the world

The Scripture firmly warns us in 1 John 2:15-17, "Love not the world, neither the things that are in the world. If any man love the world, the love of the Father is not in him. For all that is in the world, the lust of the flesh, and the lust of the eyes, and the pride of life, is not of the Father, but is of the world. And the world passeth away, and the lust thereof: but he that doeth the will of God abideth for ever."

People who love the world and its passing lusts have been systematically ensnared by the devil. The love of money, partying spirit, and night crawling to clubhouses have destroyed the souls of many.

I once had a college roommate who told me the story of his elder brother, who was coming from a party in the middle of the night, between 2:30 am and 3:30 am. On getting close to his home, he saw a group of animals, comprising dogs, sheep, goats and cats, all standing on their two feet in a circle and conversing in a human language that he could understand. His hair stood on end, the alcohol hangover in his body disappeared. He was frozen and became feverish. He ran home and was sick for three months to the point of death. When prayers were made for him, it was revealed that he had walked through the midst of the "elders in council" of his community and the landlady of their house must be appeased before he could be cured; otherwise, he was going to die. His mother desperately struggled to do all she was asked to do before the young man was eventually cured.

In essence, the spirit of partying almost killed the young man, until God had mercy on him. Young people, in particular, need to detoxify themselves of clubbing spirit, partying spirit, covetousness and greed.

7. Fleshly indulgence

There are people who cannot bear to discipline their flesh and deny it of its cravings, even when they are being spiritually stifled and endangered. Such people pamper their flesh to the detriment of their spirit man. For some people, their challenge is excessive sleep and relaxation. They can sleep for several hours, without paying attention to the Spirit's promptings to pray. As a result, all kinds of disorders and abnormalities have been introduced into their lives and families. Matthew 13:25 says, "But while men slept, his enemy came and sowed tares among the wheat, and went his way."

Proverbs 24:30-34 gives this interesting and very instructive illustration on the dangers of excessive sleep and relaxation: "I went by the field of the slothful, and by the vineyard of the man void of understanding; And, lo, it was all grown over with thorns, and nettles had covered the face thereof, and the stone wall thereof was broken down. Then I saw, and considered it well: I looked upon it, and received instruction. Yet a little sleep, a little slumber, a little folding of the hands to sleep: So shall thy poverty come as one that travelleth;and thy want as an armed man."

Other forms of fleshly indulgence that serve as spiritual toxins include gluttony (excessive eating) and addiction to fashion, luxury and vanity.

8. Pride

Pride is the oldest of spiritual toxins, being the very sin that made Satan to rebel against God, which got him expelled from heaven (Ezekiel 28:14-17). Proud people always have an exaggerated feeling of self-importance and self-worth, usually because of their natural endowments, appearance, abilities, achievements and other advantages that they think they have over others. This makes them develop a superiority complex, which reflects in their expressions, carriage, mannerisms and attitudes towards other people.

Pride is a toxin that must be eradicated from our souls before it destroys our homes, marriages, ministries, and eternal destiny. The Bible makes it pointedly clear that "God resisteth the proud, but giveth grace unto the humble" (James 4:6). We must consciously reject the toxin of pride by humbling ourselves, so that God will not have to humble us. God's humbling can be much more severe, as He reveals in Leviticus 26:19-20, "And I will break the pride of your power; and I will make your heaven as iron, and your earth as brass: And your strength shall be spent in vain: for your land shall not yield her increase, neither shall the trees of the land yield their fruits."

9. Self-will and self-ways

Proverbs 14:14 reveals that "The backslider in heart shall be filled with his own ways: and a good man shall be satisfied from himself." People who are filled with their own ways are backsliders in heart. They have their own opinion. They are Narcissistic, stubborn, opinionated, always right; every other person is always wrong and offensive to them. Such people are full of the toxins of self-ways, which often leads to self-ruin.

Spiritual detoxification will help in shifting our focus away from self-will to seeking divine instructions and yielding to God's way at all times.

10. Evil communications

Evil communications or ungodly association and companionship is a very deadly toxin that guarantees spiritual defilement and retrogression. This is clearly revealed in 1 Corinthians 15:33, "Be not deceived: evil communications corrupt good manners." It is an established fact that we sooner or later become like the people we often associate with. Invariably, then, when we associate with the godly and wise, we will cherish godliness and reflect wisdom in all we do; but when we associate with the ungodly and foolish, then our spiritual life and indeed all other areas of our lives become vulnerable to death, decay and destruction. Proverbs 13:20 asserts, "He that walketh with wise men shall be wise: but a companion of fools shall be destroyed."

PRAYERS:

1. Lord God, cleanse me from every spiritual toxin and deliver me from its entanglements.
2. Every association or congregation that I have mingled with in the past that has defiled and corrupted me, I break their yokes over my life and disengage my soul from their association and corruption, in Jesus name.
3. (Teacher prays as the Spirit leads)

STUDY 3

EFFECTS OF SPIRITUAL TOXINS

Text: Hebrews 12:1

> *"Wherefore seeing we also are compassed about with so great a cloud of witnesses, let us lay aside every weight, and the sin which doth so easily beset us, and let us run with patience the race that is set before us."*

From the medical and scientific perspective, when the body of an individual is ravaged by toxins, there are some symptoms that will manifest in his or life to show that all is not well internally. We shall be applying some of these telltale signs to our spiritual life, so we can be watchful against spiritual toxins.

1. Stress and fatigue (Psalms 51:12)

The Christian journey is naturally an interesting one because of the joy of salvation springing from the indwelling Spirit of God in the believer. Isaiah 61:10 captures this well: "I will greatly rejoice in the Lord, my soul shall be joyful in my God; for he hath clothed me with the garments of salvation, he hath covered me with the robe of righteousness, as a bridegroom decketh himself with ornaments, and as a bride adorneth herself with her jewels."

On the contrary, when a believer is ravaged by spiritual toxins, the joy of living is replaced by unexplained stress, frustration and fatigue. The individual becomes tired of living. The Christian journey becomes a burden and not a delight. To carry on in his Christian race becomes difficult and he loses the joy of salvation. This loss of the joy of salvation makes many a Christian a, easy prey for the devil. This is why King David quickly prayed to God, "Restore unto me the joy of thy salvation; and uphold me with thy free spirit" (Psalms 51:12).

2. Sloppiness, stupor and slumbers (Isaiah 56:10; Romans 11:8; 12:11)

With the damaging presence of toxins in a believer's life, the spirit of slumber, sloppiness and stupor gradually comes upon him. He is sluggish with the things of God and in the things of God. He is no longer fervent for God. He has become a sleepy Christian, who is not alive to the things of God or what God is doing around him. If he continues in this state, the glorious day of the Lord's return will come upon him unawares. This is why the Scripture warns us in 1 Thessalonians 5:6-8, "Therefore let us not sleep, as do others; but let us watch and be sober. For they that sleep sleep in the night; and they that be drunken are drunken in the night. But let us, who are of the day, be sober, putting on the breastplate of faith and love; and for an helmet, the hope of salvation."

3. Excess weights (Hebrews 12:1)

One of the most devastating effects of spiritual toxins on a believer's life and soul is the introduction of excess weights upon him, which makes it difficult for him to run the Christian race victoriously. Excess weights are sins and behaviors that easily beset us and make us inadequate or unfit for the race that is set before us. We earlier read the admonition in our text: "Wherefore seeing we also are compassed about with so great a cloud of witnesses, let us lay aside every weight, and the sin which doth so easily beset us, and let us run with patience the race that is set before us." (Hebrews 12:1).

The danger is that toxins start gradually, slowly, and little by little. When they have accumulated in our life or tolerated in our souls for a long time, that is when their effects start to become visible to other believers. We must therefore rid ourselves of the toxins of excess weights now before they disqualify us from the heavenly race and eternal rewards.

Begin to ask yourself, beloved. What are the weights in your life now?

Name then and begin to detoxify yourself through prayers by the blood of Jesus.

4. Dullness of mind (Matthew 13:15)

A life that is besieged by spiritual toxins is usually afflicted with dullness of mind. With this, the individual cannot hear, receive or understand spiritual things quickly. He cannot discern spiritual matters; he cannot pick signals in the spirit realm. Spiritual dullness has set it in. Matthew 13:15 says, "For this people's heart is waxed gross, and their ears are dull of hearing, and their eyes they have closed; lest at any time they should see with their eyes, and hear with their ears, and should understand with their heart, and should be converted, and I should heal them."

5. Spiritual cataracts and glaucoma (2 Peter 1:8-9)

Another side effect of spiritual toxins is that the affected believer begins to suffer from spiritual cataract and glaucoma. Simply put, his vision of heavenly things is impaired and distorte. 2 Peter 1:8-9 says, "For if these things be in you, and abound, they make you that ye shall neither be barren nor unfruitful in the knowledge of our Lord Jesus Christ. But he that lacketh these things is blind, and cannot see afar off, and hath forgotten that he was purged from his old sins."

Spiritual toxins make it difficult to discern or perceive when there is about to be a supernatural move of God.

The affected believer is always in haste. He only evaluates issues and matters in his life through other people's eyes and lives.

6. Partial blindness or total blindness (Romans 11:25; 1 Samuel 3:2)

It is said of Eli, the priest, in 1 Samuel 3:2, "And it came to pass at that time, when Eli was laid down in his place, and his eyes began to wax dim, that he could not see." This is what happens with spiritual toxins. Eli had allowed the toxin of fatherly indulgence to creep into his life and he seemed to regard his children above the Almighty God, such that he could not take decisive actions against them, despite repeated warning. The result was that he could no longer receive direct revelations and insights from God. This immediately made God to direct His attention to the young Samuel who eventually replaced Eli.

7. Spiritual stroke or paralysis (Ezekiel 13: 20-23)

Stroke occurs when the necessary arteries and veins carrying and supplying blood to the brain and vital organs of the body are blocked, cutting off essential blood supply. When the flow of God's life in a believer is blocked by the toxins of iniquity and bad habits, spiritual stroke and paralysis occur. Consequently, he loses spiritual stamina and vibrancy. He cannot faith anything anymore. He cannot believe the word of God anymore. He cannot hold on to the word of God anymore in the midst of challenges. He begins to look for a rod, a walking stick or a staff to lean on.

Just as it happened to Saul 1 Samuel 28:7-8, the believer that is conquered by spiritual toxins begins to rely on a medium, a fortune-teller or one with a familiar spirit to tell him what God is saying. 1 Samuel 28:7-8 says, "Then said Saul unto his servants, Seek me a woman that hath a familiar spirit, that I may go to her, and enquire of her. And his servants said to him, Behold, there is a woman that hath a familiar spirit at Endor. And Saul disguised himself, and put on other raiment, and he went, and two men with him, and they came to the woman by night: and he said, I pray thee, divine unto me by the familiar spirit, and bring me him up, whom I shall name unto thee."

That's what toxins do to someone who had once been fervent for God and violent against evil-doers. He can't believe God on his own anymore; he needs somebody to give him something to lean on or to believe in – perhaps a charm, an amulet, a talisman, or a secret book of psalms.

If you are in this state, you have suffered spiritual strokes and paralysis.

8. Spiritual thyroid dysfunction

According to Health Matters Today, the thyroid gland is a gland that is located in the neck area and is mainly responsible for producing and secreting certain hormones. These hormones are largely responsible for how energetic we are feeling, among other things.

If this gland is not producing hormones in usual quantities, for whatever reason, it can have a profound impact on us. An underactive thyroid is not necessarily dangerous, but it can have a considerable impact on the patient's life.

There are 12 signs of a dysfunctional thyroid, which we can apply to our spiritual life, as part of the effects of spiritual toxins.

1. Feeling cold. You become cold spiritually. You cannot feel or produce the heat or fire of God in you to burn up the works of Satan.

2. Dry and itchy skin. You become spiritually dry. No life of God, because you are no longer planted by the riverside of the Spirit.

3. Fatigue. You experience constant, unexplained tiredness. You complain about everything in the church - regular church services, special services, donations in church, guest ministers, and so on. It is a sign of spiritual thyroid dysfunction.

4. Constipation. Constipation is when you are taking in but not giving out according to the capacity of your intake.

5. Weight gain. You gain weight in the things of this world.

6. Hair loss (alopecia). You begin to suffer the loss of whatever anointing you have.
7. Weakness. This brings about both lethargy and vulnerability to the enemy's attacks.
8. Irregular menstruation. Things are no longer normal. You can't enjoy your normal life anymore. Even the relationship with your family is strained.
9. Foggy mind. Your mind becomes clouded and you cannot receive the word of truth anymore.
10. Depression. You begin to sink into depression and fearful hallucinations. You become paranoid.
11. Isolation. Your depression and unstable state of mind will lead you to desire isolation from holy brethren who can help you.
12. Destruction or death. This is the ultimate danger. From depression to isolation and isolation usually leads to destruction.

9. Multiple personality disorder and bipolar disorder (Mark 5:6-9)

Mark 5:6-9 narrates Jesus' encounter with the possessed man living in tombs in the city of the Gadarenes, "But when he saw Jesus afar off, he ran and worshipped him, And cried with a loud voice, and said, What have I to do with thee, Jesus, thou Son of the most high God? I adjure thee by God, that thou torment me not. For he said unto him, Come out of the man, thou unclean spirit. And he asked him, What is thy name? And he answered, saying, My name is Legion: for we are many." This man apparently had too many spiritual toxins (demonic influences) in him, and the effect was glaring – his multiple personality disorder. On the one hand, He was excited about the arrival of Jesus, but on the other hand, the demons in him made him to be worried about the idea of being delivered. They made the man restless, even to the point of harming himself.

This is what spiritual toxins also do in believers' lives. There is usually a mix-up that causes the individual to be restless, unpredictable and erratic in thinking and behavior.

10. Spiritual obesity (Revelation 3:17-18)

Toxins make us overweight and unable to run adequately. Sadly much of the weight brought about by toxins is a buildup of junk in the system. Sooner or later, there will be a breakdown, if corrective steps are not taken. Jesus told the Laodicean church: "Because thou sayest, I am rich, and increased with goods, and have need of nothing; and knowest not that thou art wretched, and miserable, and poor, and blind, and naked: I counsel thee to buy of me gold tried in the fire, that thou mayest be rich; and white raiment, that thou mayest be clothed, and that the shame of thy nakedness do not appear; and anoint thine eyes with eyesalve, that thou mayest see." (Revelation 3:17-18).

PRAYERS:

1. Heavenly Father, purge me of the roots and symptoms of toxins.
2. Oh Lord, whatever I have eaten, believed of wrongfully confessed that has affected my faith and speed in life, purge me of them in Jesus' name.
3. Lord, create a clean heart and a new spirit within me.

STUDY 4

PATHWAY TO DETOXIFICATION AND RENEWAL

TEXTS: Song of Songs 2:14; Proverbs 30:18-19

> *"O my dove, that art in the clefts of the rock, in the secret places of the stairs, let me see thy countenance, let me hear thy voice; for sweet is thy voice, and thy countenance is comely."*(Song of Songs 2:14)

> *"There be three things which are too wonderful for me, yea, four which I know not: The way of an eagle in the air; the way of a serpent upon a rock; the way of a ship amid the sea; and the way of a man with a maid." (Proverbs 30:18-19)*

To be completely cleansed and delivered from the harmful effects of spiritual toxins, we need a path that will lead to our detoxification and renewal. The detoxification business globally is worth $69.85 billion. This is an estimate of how much people spend yearly to detoxify their body and stay healthy. Yet, most of these spend little or nothing on their souls – apparently ignorant of the fact that it is a healthy soul that actually sustains the body.

In the natural world, people do not want to die; they are constantly detoxifying with all kinds of formulations in order to stay healthy. Similarly, if we are going to stay healthy spiritually, we must identify the means, ways, and substances to use in detoxifying ourselves.

AGENTS OF SPIRITUAL DETOXIFICATION

1. Fear of God and love for God

The fear God will keep you from evil and help you keep your soul pure and healthy. Psalm 119:9-10 reveals, "Wherewithal shall a young man cleanse his way? by taking heed thereto according to thy word. With my whole heart have I sought thee: O let me not wander from thy commandments."

The fear of God is of utmost importance in our lives. The truth is that our souls cannot be purer than the degree of the fear of God in us. However, in addition to the fear of God, we must also passionately love Him with all our heart, soul and might (Deuteronomy 6:5).

Now, there is a difference between the fear of God and the love of God. It is possible to love God and not fear Him. A man may love his wife, children or friends and yet not fear or reverence them. For instance, true fear of

God and reverence for your spouse will keep you from cheating on her or him.

The fear of God has to do with a special awe and honor for God. This was the kind of fear and reverence that Joseph demonstrated while being tempted by Potiphar's wife. He replied, "How then can I do this great wickedness, and sin against God?" (Genesis 39:9).

Many believers today claim to love God. We love Him enough to praise Him, worship Him, pray to Him and give to Him; but we do not fear Him enough when nobody is watching us. We do not fear Him enough to honor Him with our body parts - mouth, eyes, ears, heart and so forth. We must seriously develop a fear for God and not just a love for him alone, if we must be rid of spiritual toxins.

2. A passion for knowing and doing God's word

Psalm 19:7 says, "The law of the Lord is perfect, converting the soul: the testimony of the Lord is sure, making wise the simple."

We have many people who claim to know about God and His word. In fact, some know the word so much that they can recite it by heart and rhyme it at night when going to bed or when in danger. But few obey the word or allow it to control their lives.

For instance, the Scripture says, " He that covereth a

transgression seeketh love; but he that repeateth a matter separateth very friends." (Proverbs 17:9). But, in reality, how many believers can intentionally choose to overlook a wrong or cover a wrong? While we must not condone or indulge anyone in evil, it is better to choose to let go of personal hurts, so that there may be peace. This is especially important in a relationship, marriage and in the church of God where we serve. Most of the grievances we hold on to and repeat do not produce any works of righteousness; rather, they lead to more strife.

Knowing and doing God's word will continually purify and keep our souls pure, while also renewing our spiritual strength.

3. Prayer and fasting

Prayer is an act of communion between God and man. It is the divine funnel by which God pours His liquid fire to purify our souls and re-ignite our heart with a new love and fear for Him. When we pray, the dross (toxins) in us is constantly cleansed by the blood of His Son, Jesus Christ. Ephesians 1:7 assures, "In whom we have redemption through his blood, the forgiveness of sins, according to the riches of his grace."

Through prayers in Jesus' name, we have redemption and forgiveness of our sins. We are purged from every toxin of the soul. The Holy Spirit points to us the dross in our heart and He releases His fire and power to burn it off. Proverbs 25:4-5 declares, " Take away the dross from the silver, and there shall come forth a vessel for the finer. Take away the wicked from before the king, and his throne shall be established in righteousness."

Fasting, on the other hand, helps us to subdue the works and activity of the flesh. Fasting hastens the process of cleansing. It helps to quickly draw our soul closer to God and our spirit is humbled to receive the works of the refiner. Malachi 3:3 describes the cleansing process, "And he shall sit as a refiner and purifier of silver: and he shall purify the sons of Levi, and purge them as gold and silver, that they may offer unto the Lord an offering in righteousness."

Beyond the purification of our soul, fasting also helps to cleanse and recharge our body. This is why fasting must always go with prayer and the control of the word of God; otherwise, there may be serious problems. The truth is that after a long fast, your soul is purified and your hormones are renewed and restored. This is the reason many people who engage in long fasting without prayers and control by the word end up being highly sexually immoral. Therefore, we must always balance our life and work with Him, in Him and by Him and His Holy Ghost renewal in us. "Not by works of righteousness which we have done, but according to His mercy He saved us, by the washing of regeneration, and renewing of the Holy Ghost" (Titus 3:5)

It is important that we fast with purpose and understanding. Fasting must never be for competition; rather, it must be done with the knowledge of God, as well as control and accountability.

4. Waiting like the eagle

The ways of the eagle are truly unique. The eagle soars, glides and mounts up higher when running away from the enemy. Indeed, the eagle is the only bird that can look directly at the sun. The enemy birds chasing it cannot look at the sun; it will go blind. When the enemies chase the eagle, it looks at the sun and is able to mount up higher, while the enemies turn back.

In the same way, to be spiritually renewed, we must continually look unto the Sun of Righteousness, Jesus Christ. When we do, our sight is purified, restored and renewed. God has promised us in Malachi 4:2, "But unto you that fear my name shall the Sun of righteousness arise with healing in his wings; and ye shall go forth, and grow up as calves of the stall."

Learning from the eagle's gaze at the sun, we keep staring at Jesus, and thereby keep soaring higher. This helps to detoxify our souls and renew our spiritual strength. With this, we can do more for God and see more with Him and through Him.

PRAYERS

1. Father, take me to the secret place of your purging.
2. Father, make me clean and pure and give me a new wing to be able to soar in Jesus' name.
3. Lord God, help me to keep my gaze on the Sun of Righteousness for daily cleansing and renewal.

STUDY 5

OVERCOMING SPIRITUAL TOXINS OF SMYRNA

Text: Revelation 2:8-11

> *"And unto the angel of the church in Smyrna write; These things saith the first and the last, which was dead, and is alive; I know thy works, and tribulation, and poverty, (but thou art rich) and I know the blasphemy of them which say they are Jews, and are not, but are the synagogue of Satan. Fear none of those things which thou shalt suffer: behold, the devil shall cast some of you into prison, that ye may be tried; and ye shall have tribulation ten days: be thou faithful unto death, and I will give thee a crown of life.*

He that hath an ear, let him hear what the Spirit saith unto the churches; He that overcometh shall not be hurt of the second death."

John the Beloved penned this letter, as directed by Jesus Christ, to commend the recipients for their endurance of persecution and poverty for the sake of the gospel. He also did so to exhort them to be fearless and faithful even unto death. Whereas the Ephesian church needed to return to their first love, the church in Smyrna needed to persevere in what was characteristic of their persecution in the present circumstances.

DESTINATION AND DESCRIPTION OF CHRIST

The church in Smyrna was not just an ordinary local church; it was a church located in a bubbling and thriving city at that time. It was located in the hubs of activity and merchandising in the then world.

Smyrna was a seaport on the Aegean Sea. It stood about 40 miles north of Ephesus. Late in the first century, it was a large wealthy city with a population of about 100,000 people or more. It still thrives today as Izmir, the third most populous city in Turkey and the country's largest port after Istanbul, with a population of about 2.6 million people.

The revelation of Jesus Christ to the Smyrna church was that He described Himself as the Eternal One who died and resurrected. Here is Revelation 2:8 again, "And unto the angel of the church in Smyrna write; These things saith the first and the last, which was dead, and is alive." This introduction was very significant for the believers in Smyrna. These believers would have found encouragement in the fact that, even though the suffering of persecution and the possibility of death threatened them, resurrection and eternal life with Christ were certain.

It is equally important to know that the name "Smyrna" means "Bitter." Accordingly, it can be deduced that this church had learned through persecution how to eat the bitter things of the Spirit to purge their souls from the corruption that was in the world. They were unlike their counterparts, the Laodicean church, who loved the sweet things of life, and equated such with prosperity, not knowing that they were actually consuming toxins that could lead them to eternal death (Revelation 3:14-19).

Moreover, the reality that the church in Smyrna, as their name implies, were eating bitterness and purging their souls, reminds us of a cardinal truth about our faith: Those who will live godly in Christ Jesus must suffer persecution. Apostle Paul charged Timothy, in 2 Timothy 3:10-13, "But thou hast fully known my doctrine, manner of life, purpose, faith, longsuffering, charity, patience… Yea, and all that will live godly in Christ Jesus shall suffer persecution. But evil men and seducers shall wax worse and worse, deceiving, and being deceived."

CHRIST'S COMMENDATION

"I know thy works, and tribulation, and poverty, (but thou art rich) and I know the blasphemy of them which say they are Jews, and are not, but are the synagogue of Satan." (Revelation 2:9).

Jesus Christ knew the afflictions and pressures that the Smyrnan Christians were experiencing as a result of their testimony for Him. These included abject poverty. Evidently, their persecutors were cutting off some of their means of survival. However, despite their physical poverty, the Smyrnan Christians were rich spiritually. Beloved, what shall separate us from the love of Christ? Persecution or death? Nay, none of these things.

It is also apparent that some of the persecutors of the Smyrnan believers were Jews. Acts 18:12-17 says "And when Gallio was the deputy of Achaia, the Jews made insurrection with one accord against Paul, and brought him to the judgment seat, Saying, This fellow persuadeth men to worship God contrary to the law. And when Paul was now about to open his mouth, Gallio said unto the Jews, If it were a matter of wrong or wicked lewdness, O ye Jews, reason would that I should bear with you: But if it be a question of words and names, and of your law, look ye to it ; for I will be no judge of such matters. [16] And he drave them from the judgment seat. Then all the Greeks took Sosthenes, the chief ruler of the synagogue, and beat him before the judgment seat. And Gallio cared for none of those things."

The church in Smyrna was persecuted by leaders and people who claimed they know God. They claimed to be committed to God but were not. They came out of Satan's camp. They were toxins in the feast of the church (Acts 14:19; 17:5-8, 13).

Jesus Christ had no rebuke for the saints in Smyrna. They

were obviusly above board. Evidently, in their trials, they had remained pure in belief and behavior. God wants us to remain absolutely unbroken and undefiled by the rotten gospel of pleasures of this age.

TIMELY ADMONITION

The Smyrnan church were charged in Revelation 2:10, "Fear none of those things which thou salt suffer: behold, the devil shall cast some of you into prison, that ye may be tried; and ye shall have tribulation ten days: be thou faithful unto death, and I will give thee a crown of life."

The persecuted Christians did not need to fear their adversaries or death, since they would live forever with Jesus Christ. The "ten days" of trouble may refer to a period of relatively brief duration, specifically the "days" of persecution under Roman emperors. There is nothing in the text that provides a clue that we should take this number in a figurative sense.

CHEERING PROMISE

"Fear none of those things which thou shalt suffer: behold, the devil shall cast some of you into prison, that ye may be tried; and ye shall have tribulation ten days: be thou faithful unto death, and I will give thee a crown of life. He that hath an ear, let him hear what the Spirit saith unto the churches; He that overcometh shall not be hurt of the second death." (Revelation 2:10-11)

The crown of life is the victor's crown given for enduring the trials and tests of life, even to the point of death, without denying Christ. It is not the gift of eternal life but the fullness of that life (cf. John 10:10, et al.). The person who endures these trials will receive this crown after Jesus Christ has approved him or her. (1 Corinthians 3:13-14.) The first death might hurt them briefly, but the second death will not hurt them at all.

CENTRAL TRUTH

Suffering for Christ's sake is part of the conditions for entering into the Kingdom of Heaven. (Acts14:22; 2 Corinthians 4:17; 1 Peter 4:13)

Sometimes, afflictions, sorrows and persecutions help to purge the spiritual toxins of life from a believer's life. Trials and persecutions help to keep us sound and in good standing in our faith in God. King David shared his experience thus: "It is good for me that I have been afflicted; that I might learn thy statutes." (Psalm 119:71)

We do not pray for afflictions, because they will naturally come; but we pray for strength to survive afflictions and we prepare strength for and before the days of affliction.

Lastly, if we are going to be strong and reign with him, we must settle it in our mind that in order to reign with Him, we must suffer with Him. "It is a faithful saying: For if we be dead with him, we shall also live with him: If we suffer, we shall also reign with him: if we deny him, he also will deny us." (2 Timothy 2:11-12).

PRAYERS

1. Lord, I receive the grace to be able to suffer and endure all things for the sake of Christ.
2. Lord, help me to love you with all I am and all I have.
3. Father, help me to stand for you, no matter the challenges to my faith.

STUDY 6

BELIEVERS'TRIALS AND TRIUMPH

TEXT: Revelation 2:8-11; Job 23: 10

"And unto the angel of the church in Smyrna write; These things saith the first and the last, which was dead, and is alive; I know thy works, and tribulation, and poverty, (but thou art rich) and I know the blasphemy of them which say they are Jews, and are not, but are the synagogue of Satan. Fear none of those things which thou shalt suffer: behold, the devil shall cast some of you into prison, that ye may be tried; and ye shall have tribulation ten days: be thou faithful unto death, and I will give thee a crown of life. He that hath an ear, let him hear what the Spirit saith unto the churches, He that overcometh shall not be hurt of the second death. (Revelation 2:8-11)

"But he knoweth the way that I take: when he hath tried me, I shall come forth as gold." (Job 23:10)

> *Believers are positionally in the royal family of God, having been born again by God through the Holy Spirit. One day, we shall receive our glorified body and be like the eternal Son of God (1 John 3:1-3).*

Notwithstanding, at the initial stage, our walk of faith usually proves difficult, with many friends and loved ones opposing and deserting us. (Matthew 10:22; Luke 21:17; John 15:18-25). This is expected because when God the Holy Spirit gives us a new birth, we become different from the people of the world (2 Corinthians 4:4). With this newness of life comes persecution and trials, which serve different useful purposes for our heavenly journey.

SCRIPTURAL PERSPECTIVES ON TRIALS

Let us consider a few Bible references concerning the kinds of trials that believers face today in the world. This is necessary so that when these difficulties and problems come your way, you do not think that you are a failure in your Christian walk. Many a time, great trials come to those who want to be useful to the Lord. Ephesians 6:12 reminds us that "we wrestle not against flesh and blood, but against principalities, against powers, against the rulers of the darkness of this world, against spiritual wickedness in high places."

Consider these examples

1. God allowed Job to be tried – Job 1:1-12; 2:1-8, 23:10; 9:23

- Job was a righteous man
- Job was a wealthy man
- Job had an unsympathetic wife
- Job had critical friends
- Job knew that someday he would see God
- Job believed in the resurrection

2. Abraham was tried:

- Through Ishmael, the result of trying to help God with His promises. To this very day, the descendants of Ishmael give the Hebrew people trouble.
- Sarah was barren
- Isaac was to be offered up to God – Hebrews 11:17-19; Genesis 22:1-14
- Abraham looked for the city which God would build but died waiting – Hebrews 11:10

3. Noah's faith was tried when his preaching brought no results from the people

- The hard work of building an ark as the people laughed.

- Telling of rain which had never been seen before.
- No doubt, some of his relatives left him, thinking that he was insane.

Also:

- Paul the Apostle had a thorn in the flesh – 2 Corinthians 12:7
- Timothy had frequent upset stomach – 1 Timothy 5:23
- Jacob wrestled with an angel and was afflicted – Genesis 32:24-32
- Daniel was thrown into the lions' den – Daniel 6:1-28
- Christ suffered afflictions for us – Isaiah 53:1-10; Psalm 22:1-31, Matthew 27:27-50; Mark 15:16-23; Luke 23:26-32; John 1916-17

Trials of fire – Psalm 12:6; 17:3; 66:10; Daniel 12:10; Zechariah 13:9; Revelation 3:18

(1) Shadrach, Meshach, and Abednego – Daniel 3:8-30

(2) Saints of great faith – (Hebrews 11:32-34).

(3) Our works as believers are to be tried by fire – 1 Corinthians 3:9-16; 2 Corinthians 5:10

We must expect to suffer for the cause of Christ – I

Thessalonians 2:1-5; we must also learn to rejoice with our victorious Lord in His suffering for us (Philippians 3:10).

THE TRIALS OF OUR FAITH

As a professing Christian, what you believe and stand for will be tried. Your faith and holiness will be tried. However, you must never tempt God in your trials, as a believer. Many believers in the time of their trials try God by giving Him conditions, such as: "if I am not free from this affliction before next week Monday, I will kill myself and die off."

Such expressions do not move God nor make Him change His mind. Some people will even tell God in their complaints (not prayers) "If really you are God, heal me now or I die." The truth, however, is that whether you live or die does not add or take away from God. He remains God forever. So, try to avoid tempting God in the days of your trials (Psalm 78:18-56; 95:9; 106:14).

You must understand that:

(A) God does not tempt us but rather tries us – James 1:13-14

(B) We are tempted by Satan – Matthew 4:3, 1 Thessalonians 3:5, Mark 1:3, Luke 4:2

TRIUMPHING OVER TRIALS

Any believer who would overcome trials when it comes must learn to put on and deploy these weapons:

1. Weapon of the word

- The Word of God is our lifeline – Acts 15:35; 18:11; 28:31, Colossians 1:28; 3:16.
- The Word of God is powerful – Hebrews 4:12.
- God, the Holy Spirit, will guide you through God's Word – Isaiah 48:16; Romans 8:14.
- God, the Holy Spirit, provides power over sin through God's Word – Zechariah 4:6.
- God is always ready to deliver you whenever you call upon Him through His Word – 2 Peter 2:9.

2. Weapon of prayers

The words of the popular song are true - Prayer is the key; prayer is one of the master keys, Jesus started with prayer and ended with prayer. (Mark 11:24, 1 John 5:14-15, Matthew 7:7-8, 2 Chronicles 7:14, 1 Thessalonians 5:16-17; Jeremiah 29:12).

Prayer will fetch you the necessary strength and grace you need to keep going on, regardless of the enemies' onslaughts.

3. Weapon of praise

This is a way to glorify God no matter what your need may be. A time of trial is a time to remember all your benefits in Christ Jesus. At least you are alive; that is why you know you have other needs. So, say good things about God. (Exodus 15:2, Psalm 119:175, Ephesians 1:12, 1 Chronicles 20:21-23).

4. Weapon of thanksgiving

In 1 Chronicles 20:21, Jehoshaphat and his also used the weapon of thanksgiving to fight their enemies in times of trials. When you are confronted with trials, learn to give thanks to God, for the Bible says it is good to do so. (Psalm 118:1; 1 Chronicles 16:8; Psalm 100:4, 1 Corinthians 15:57, 1 Thessalonians 5:18).

CONCLUSION

Believers should always remember that Christ Himself was tried in all points as we are today (Luke 4:13; 10:25, Hebrews 2:18; 4:15). We will have trials, as long as we are in this world and in our present fleshly body. The Lord has given us the proper armor to protect us against the wiles of the devil, and may we use them at all times. Ephesians 6:13 says, "Wherefore take unto you the whole armor of God, that ye may be able to withstand in the evil day, and having done all, to stand."

As believers with the Holy Spirit within us, we have a tremendous capacity to withstand the world, the flesh and the devil because God is sovereign, and we are dependent upon God the Holy Spirit at each stage of our trials.

PRAYERS:

1. Lord, we pray for all persecuted believers worldwide; give them the grace to stand for you always.
2. Father, help me to stand for you in spite of any opposition or trials of my faith.
3. Strengthen me, Lord, so as not to faint in the days of adversity.

STUDY 7

TOXINS THAT KILL FIRST LOVE

Text: Revelation 2:1-7

"Unto the angel of the church of Ephesus write; These things saith he that holdeth the seven stars in his right hand, who walketh in the midst of the seven golden candlesticks; I know thy works, and thy labor, and thy patience, and how thou canst not bear them which are evil: and thou hast tried them which say they are apostles, and are not, and hast found them liars: And hast borne, and hast patience, and for my name's sake hast labored, and hast not fainted. Nevertheless I have somewhat against thee, because thou hast left thy first love. Remember therefore from whence thou art fallen, and repent, and do the first works; or else I will come unto thee quickly, and will remove thy candlestick out of his place, except thou repent. But this thou hast, that thou hatest the deeds of the Nicolaitans, which I also hate. He that hath an ear, let him hear what the Spirit saith unto the churches; To him that overcometh will I give to eat of the tree of life, which is in the midst of the paradise of God."

The Lord Jesus told John to write a letter to the church in Ephesus to commend them for their labors and perseverance in God's truth. He also wanted to exhort them to rekindle their former love for the Savior because certain toxins of life had affected the first love of this church for their Savior and first Husband.

DESTINATION AND DESCRIPTION OF CHRIST

"Unto the angel of the church of Ephesus write; These things saith he that holdeth the seven stars in his right hand, who walketh in the midst of the seven golden candlesticks" (Revelation 2:1).

Ephesus was a leading seaport and the capital of the Roman province of Asia. Paul had evangelized it and used it as a base of operations for at least three years (Acts 18:19-21;19; 1 Corinthians 16:8). Timothy had labored there (1 Timothy 1:3) as had the Apostle John. It was the largest city in Asia Minor.

The "angel" who was the primary recipient of this letter was probably the Ephesians church leader or pastor. He would have made the letter known to the congregation when he read it publicly. John described Jesus Christ figuratively as the One in authority over the churches' leaders; and One who knew their situations. He was watching over them (cf. 1:13, 16).

DIVINE COMMENDATION (Revelation 2:2-3 (cf. v. 6)

"I know thy works, and thy labor, and thy patience, and how thou canst not bear them which are evil: and thou hast tried them which say they are apostles, and are not, and hast found them liars: And hast borne, and hast patience, and for my name's sake hast labored, and hast not fainted."

The Ephesian church had remained faithful to Jesus Christ for over 40 years. He approved of the good works of these believers—their toil in His service, patient endurance of circumstances under affliction, and discipline of evil men and false teachers.

POIGNANT REBUKE (Revelation 2:4)

"Nevertheless I have somewhat against thee, because thou hast left thy first love."

Despite their uncommon devotion, the Ephesians were serving Jesus Christ and maintaining orthodoxy and tradition, rather than serving God out of fervent love for their Savior (cf. Ephesians 1:15-16). They did what was right but for the wrong reason. They were serving and worshipping for shows off, appraisals of men and earthly rewards. Their service was not born out of passion and fervent love for the master.

Service and orthodoxy are important, but Jesus Christ

wants our passionate love too. 'It is only as we love Christ fervently that we can serve Him faithfully.' "Howbeit in vain do they worship Me, teaching for doctrines the commandments of men. [8] For laying aside the commandment of God, ye hold the tradition of men, as the washing of pots and cups: and many other such like things ye do. [9] And He said unto them, Full well ye reject the commandment of God, that ye may keep your own tradition." (Mark 7:7-9).

REMEDIAL EXHORTATION (Revelation 2:5-6)

"Remember therefore from whence thou art fallen, and repent, and do the first works; or else I will come unto thee quickly, and will remove thy candlestick out of his place, except thou repent. But this thou hast, that thou hatest the deeds of the Nicolaitans, which I also hate."

The correction for a cold heart that the Lord prescribed was a three-step process.

1. We need to remember how we used to feel about Him, to repent (change our attitude), and return to the love that formerly motivated us. The "first works" most likely refers to the activities that fanned the flame of our love (e.g. Personal prayer time with Him, fasting, evangelism, devotion, personal night vigil, avoiding and running away from iniquity, and so on).

2. To rekindle our first love, there needs to be a return to our first works because there is an intimate relationship

between love and good works (1 John 5:2). The church that loses its love will soon lose its light, no matter how doctrinally sound it may be. Eventually the Ephesian church passed out of existence, but that did not occur until the fifth century.

The recipients of this letter seemed to have responded positively to this exhortation. Moreover, it is interesting to note that while they had left their first love, they had not left their former hatred for evil – as represented by "the deeds of the Nicolaitans". We know little of the Nicolaitans who were followers of someone evidently named Nicolas (cf. Acts 6:5). Irenaeus, who lived in the late second century, wrote that the Nicolaitans were without restraint in their indulgence of the flesh, as they freely practiced fornication and ate foods sacrificed to idols.

Also noteworthy is that the word "Nicolaitans" is a transliteration of two Greek words that mean "to conquer" and "people." Consequently, "Nicolaitans" has come down through history as typifying any system that seeks to dominate rather than serve people.

AFFECTIONATE PROMISE (Revelation 2:7)

"He that hath an ear, let him hear what the Spirit saith unto the churches; To him that overcometh will I give to eat of the tree of life, which is in the midst of the paradise of God."

Christ concluded his message to the Ephesian church with a special promise that was meant to assure them of His continued affection here and in eternity, if they would repent and heed His rebuke. The special invitation that preceded the promise – "He that hath an ear, let him hear" - is very significant. Indeed, Jesus was the first and only person to issue this invitation in Scripture. The Gospels also record Him doing so seven times (Matthew 11:15; 13:9, 43; Mark 4:9, 23; Luke 8:8; 14:35). This invitation always occurs where Jesus appealed to His hearers to make a significant change.

Jesus Christ gave a promise to the individuals in the church. - "Him who overcomes"- (cf. vv. 2-3, 10c, 13, 19, 25; 3:3, 8, 10; 1 John 5:4-5). Those who remember, repent, and repeat the first works (v. 5) will partake of the tree of life.

There is a connection between the tree of life and man's rule over the earth. Adam in his unfallen state had access to this tree, but when he fell, God kept him from it (Genesis1:26-28; 3:22).

In the future, believers will have access to it again (cf. 22:14)."The tree of life" reserved for believers is associated peculiarly with a provision for those who will rule and reign as co-heirs with Christ.

CENTRAL TRUTH

Your service to God should be primarily and continually motivated by your love for Him. Love is the more excellent way to serve God (1Corinthians 12:31; 13:13).

Toxins that kill love for God are:

1. Love of the world - 1 John 2:15-16
2. Friendship with the world - James 4:4
3. Lust of the flesh – Galatians 5:16
4. Pride of life - 1John 2:15-16
5. Deceitfulness of riches – Mark 4:19
6. The traditions of men - Mark 7:8
7. The commandments of men – Mark 7:7
8. Offenses - Hebrews 12:15
9. Negligence of divine purpose - Acts 26:19
10. Passivity and wrong associations - Hebrew 6:12
11. Prayerlessness. - Psalm 14:1-4
12. Neglect of fellowship with the brethren - Hebrews 10:25

PRAYER

1. Father, restore my first love for you.
2. Lord, whatever that I have loved more than you, deliver me from it or him/her.
3. Holy Spirit awaken my true love and sincere undying agape love for You.
4. Lord, I am sorry because I have let the things of this world and the cares of this life choke my love for You.
5. Lord, plant a new love and fear of You in my heart.

STUDY 8

THE PHILADELPHIAN CHRISTIAN

TEXT: Revelation 3:7-13

"And to the angel of the church in Philadelphia write; These things saith he that is holy, he that is true, he that hath the key of David, he that openeth, and no man shutteth; and shutteth, and no man openeth; I know thy works: behold, I have set before thee an open door, and no man can shut it: for thou hast a little strength, and hast kept my word, and hast not denied my name. Behold, I will make them of the synagogue of Satan, which say they are Jews, and are not, but do lie; behold, I will make them to come and worship before thy feet, and to know that I have loved thee. Because thou hast kept the word of my patience, I also will keep thee from the hour of temptation, which shall come upon all the world, to try them that dwell upon the earth. Behold, I come quickly: hold that fast which thou hast, that no man take thy crown. Him that overcometh will I make a pillar in the temple of my God, and he shall go no more out: and I will write upon him the name of my God, and the name of the city of my God, which is new Jerusalem, which cometh down out of heaven

from my God: and I will write upon him my new name. He that hath an ear, let him hear what the Spirit saith unto the churches."

The Lord sent this letter to the church in Philadelphia to praise them for their faithfulness in service, despite persecution, and to encourage them to persevere.

DESTINATION AND DESCRIPTION OF CHRIST (Revelation 3:7)

"And to the angel of the church in Philadelphia write; These things saith he that is holy, he that is true, he that hath the key of David, he that openeth, and no man shutteth; and shutteth, and no man openeth."

The word "Philadelphia" means "Brotherly Love" (cf. Romans 12:10; 1 Thessalonians 4:9; Hebrews 13:1; et al.) This city lay about 30 miles southeast of Sardis. Jesus Christ presented Himself to these saints as "holy" and the "key of David". In saying this, He made it clear that He has God's full administrative authority to distribute or not distribute all God's resources according to His will.

UPLIFTING COMMENDATION (Revelation 3:8)

"I know thy works: behold, I have set before thee an open door, and no man can shut it: for thou hast a little strength, and hast kept my word, and hast not denied my name."

The Philadelphia Christians had received an "open door", signifying an opportunity for spiritual blessing - perhaps an opportunity for evangelism. This opportunity would continue because they had a little "power" (spiritual power) though they were evidently few. They had faithfully obeyed God's Word, and had maintained a faithful testimony for the Lord in the past, presumably by word and by deed.

They also enjoyed the prospect of an open door into the Messianic Kingdom because they had been faithful. This may be the primary reference in view.

PRECIOUS PROMISES (Revelation 3:9-12)

It is worthy of note that the Lord Jesus Christ gave no rebuke to this church, as was true of the church in Smyrna. Instead, He gave them the following five promises that are equally applicable to all believers that would emulate their commendable example:

1. Their Jewish antagonists would eventually have to acknowledge that the believers were the true followers of God (cf. 2:9). These foes claimed to be the true followers of God, but they were not, having rejected Jesus Christ (cf. John 8:31-59).

2. They would escape the Great Tribulation coming upon the world.

3. They would receive a crown of commendation at the Lord's return.
4. They would be permanently established as pillars in God's heavenly temple.
5. The name of God and that of the heavenly Jerusalem would be inscribed on them.

CONCLUSION

The Philadelphian Christians were faithful in their service and love for God. Despite the challenges and persecution of their faith, they maintained steadfastness in Christ. We must emulate their example and go even deeper in our commitment to God and His service.

PRAYERS

1. Lord, I know that sometimes my strength is small, and I feel like giving up, but I ask for the grace to keep going on in my faith walk with you.
2. Father, strengthen me with power and might in my inner man, in Jesus' name.
3. Father, give me love and strength to strengthen my fellow brethren in the faith.

STUDY 9

OVERCOMING THE SPIRITUAL TOXINS OF THYATIRA

Text: Revelation 2:18-29

"And unto the angel of the church in Thyatira write; These things saith the Son of God, who hath his eyes like unto a flame of fire, and his feet are like fine brass; I know thy works, and charity, and service, and faith, and thy patience, and thy works; and the last to be more than the first. Notwithstanding I have a few things against thee, because thou sufferest that woman Jezebel, which calleth herself a prophetess, to teach and to seduce my servants to commit fornication, and to eat things sacrificed unto idols. And I gave her space to repent of her fornication; and she repented not. Behold, I will cast her into a bed, and them that commit adultery with her into great tribulation, except they repent of their deeds. And I will kill her children with death; and all the churches shall know that I am he which searcheth the reins and hearts: and I will give unto every one of you according to your works. But unto you I say, and unto the rest in Thyatira, as many as have not this

doctrine, and which have not known the depths of Satan, as they speak; I will put upon you none other burden. But that which ye have already hold fast till I come. And he that overcometh, and keepeth my works unto the end, to him will I give power over the nations: And he shall rule them with a rod of iron; as the vessels of a potter shall they be broken to shivers: even as I received of my Father. And I will give him the morning star. He that hath an ear, let him hear what the Spirit saith unto the churches."

Jesus Christ sent this letter to commend some in this church for their service, orthodoxy, and fidelity; as well as to warn others in it to turn from false teaching and sinful practices.

DESTINATION AND DESCRIPTION OF CHRIST (Revelation 2:18)

"And unto the angel of the church in Thyatira write; These things saith the Son of God, who hath his eyes like unto a flame of fire, and his feet are like fine brass."

Thyatira was the smallest of the seven cities in which the seven churches addressed in John's letters were located; yet it received the longest letter. The city lay about 45 miles to the southeast of Pergamum. It was famous for its textiles, especially the production of a purple dye (cf. Acts 16:14), and its trade guilds.

Jesus appeared here with flame-like eyes, suggesting discerning and severe judgment (cf. 1:14). Burnished (highly reflective) bronze feet in this context portrays a warrior with protected feet. (cf.1:15; Dan. 10:6). "Son of God" emphasizes Jesus Christ's deity and right to judge.

MERITED COMMENDATION (Revelation 2:19)

"I know thy works, and charity, and service, and faith, and thy patience, and thy works; and the last to be more than the first."

In many ways, some in this church were praiseworthy. They were strong in good deeds, love for others, trust in God, service of their Savior, and patient endurance in trials. Moreover, they had become even more zealous recently.

Love shows itself in service, and faith demonstrates itself in perseverance through persecution.

UNSPARING REBUKE (Revelation 2:20-23)

"Notwithstanding I have a few things against thee, because thou sufferest that woman Jezebel, which calleth herself a prophetess, to teach and to seduce my servants to commit fornication, and to eat things sacrificed unto idols. And I gave her space to repent of her fornication; and she repented not. Behold, I will cast her into a bed, and them that commit adultery with her into great tribulation, except they repent of their deeds. And I will kill her children with death; and all the churches shall know that I am he which searcheth the reins and hearts: and I will give unto every one of you according to your works."

Evidently, a woman claiming to be a prophetess (cf. Luke 2:36; Acts 21:9; 1 Corinthians 11:5), had been influencing some in this church to indulge in immoral acts and the worship of idols. Her name may or may not have been Jezebel. However, her behavior reflected that of wicked Queen Jezebel (1 Kings 16—2 Kings 9) who led Israel into immorality and idolatry by advocating Baal worship (cf. v. 14; Acts 15:28-29). God had not brought judgment on her previously so she might repent (2 Peter 3:9). However, since she refused to change her ways, God would judge her and her followers unless they repented. She might experience a fatal illness (cf. 2 Kings 1:4; 1 Corinthians 11:29-30), and her followers might experience great tribulation. Death would also be the punishment of her spiritual children (v. 23), another way of describing her followers (v. 22). The other churches would recognize her punishment as coming from God who knows all people intimately (cf. Psalm 7:9; Proverbs 24:12; Jeremiah 11:20; 17:10; 20:12).

INVIGORATING EXHORTATION (Revelation 2:24-25)

"But unto you I say, and unto the rest in Thyatira, as many

as have not this doctrine, and which have not known the depths of Satan, as they speak; I will put upon you none other burden. But that which ye have already hold fast till I come."

Apparently, the Jezebel woman claimed that her teaching (that Christians can indulge the flesh with impunity) was deeper than the apostles' teaching, but it was, of course, the depths of satanic doctrine. Jesus Christ exhorted the faithful in the church to continue with their present good conduct (v. 19). He would soon purge the wicked ones from their midst.

UNFAILING PROMISES (Revelation 2:26-29)

"And he that overcometh, and keepeth my works unto the end, to him will I give power over the nations: And he shall rule them with a rod of iron; as the vessels of a potter shall they be broken to shivers: even as I received of my Father. And I will give him the morning star. He that hath an ear, let him hear what the Spirit saith unto the churches."

The prize for faithfulness was the privilege of reigning with Christ in His earthly kingdom (cf. 1:6; 12:5; 19:15; Psalm 2:8-9; 2 Timothy 2:12; Revelation 20:4-6). As with the promises in the other letters, this one is probably for all believers and would encourage them to overcome the temptations this Jezebel held out. The Lord intended the prospect of this blessing to motivate the unfaithful in the church to return to God's will for them and to encourage the faithful to persevere.

Believers who are faithful will receive authority in heaven from Jesus Christ and will "rule" (lit. shepherd) others during the Millennium (Luke 19:11-27; 1 Corinthians 6:2-3; 2 Timothy 2:12; Revelation 3:21). Some believers evidently will receive greater authority for being faithful than others who have not been as faithful (cf. 2 Corinthians 5:10). This is the first mention in Revelation of the Lord's coming for the church, the Rapture (cf. 1 Thessalonians 4:13-18).

John identified the "morning star" (v.28) elsewhere as Jesus Christ Himself (Revelation 22:16). Jesus Christ will guide faithful believers in the future as the new day of His rule dawns (cf. Titus 2:13). A special close relationship with Jesus Christ seems to be the focus of this blessing.

CENTRAL TRUTH

Jesus is coming very soon; only those who are faithful to the end shall reign with Him.

PRAYERS

1. Father, deliver me from every wine of Jezebel that has intoxicated me or that I have drunk at any point of my life.
2. Father, purge me of every compromise of my faith that will not allow me to see Jesus.
3. Father, keep me from falling into the control, manipulations, and witchcraft of the Jezebels of these end times.

STUDY 10

CONQUERING THE SPIRITUAL TOXINS OF PERGAMOS

Text: Revelation 2:12-17

> *"And to the angel of the church in Pergamos write; These things saith he which hath the sharp sword with two edges; I know thy works, and where thou dwellest, even where Satan's seat is: and thou holdest fast my name, and hast not denied my faith, even in those days wherein Antipas was my faithful martyr, who was slain among you, where Satan dwelleth. But I have a few things against thee, because thou hast there them that hold the doctrine of Balaam, who taught Balac to cast a stumblingblock before the children of Israel, to eat things sacrificed unto idols, and to commit fornication. So hast thou also them that hold the doctrine of the Nicolaitans, which thing I hate. Repent; or else I will come unto thee quickly, and will fight against them with the sword of my mouth. He that hath an ear, let him hear what the Spirit saith unto the churches; To him that overcometh will I give to eat of the hidden manna, and will give him a white stone, and in the*

stone a new name written, which no man knoweth saving he that receiveth it."

The purpose of this letter was to commend the Christians in Pergamos for their faithfulness to Christ and to urge them to reject the false and toxic teachings in their midst.

DESTINATION AND DESCRIPTION OF CHRIST (Revelation 2:12)

"And to the angel of the church in Pergamos write; These things saith he which hath the sharp sword with two edges."

Pergamos (modern Bergama) lay about 55 miles north of Smyrna inland, a few miles from the Aegean coast. The meaning of the name "Pergamos" is "Citadel." The town was noteworthy for three reasons. One, it was a center for many pagan religious cults, and emperor worship was more intense there than in any other surrounding city. Two, it boasted a university with a large library. Three, it was the center for the production of parchments.

Jesus Christ described Himself as the One who judges with His Word (cf. 1:16; 19:15, 21). God's Word separates believers from the world and sinners from God. This is perhaps its double-edged quality.

FITTING COMMENDATION (Revelation 2:13)

"I know thy works, and where thou dwellest, even where Satan's seat is: and thou holdest fast my name, and hast not denied my faith, even in those days wherein Antipas was my faithful martyr, who was slain among you, where Satan dwelleth."

The Pergamos Christians had held firmly to their commitment to Jesus Christ and had been effective witnesses for Him, even though they lived in one of Satan's strongholds. "Satan's seat" may be an allusion to one or more of the pagan temples in the city.

STERN REBUKE (2:14-15)

"But I have a few things against thee, because thou hast there them that hold the doctrine of Balaam, who taught Balac to cast a stumblingblock before the children of Israel, to eat things sacrificed unto idols, and to commit fornication. So hast thou also them that hold the doctrine of the Nicolaitans, which thing I hate."

The pagans in Pergamos were evidently encouraging the Christians to join in their pagan feasts and the sexual immorality that accompanied them. The Nicolaitans evidently regarded these sins as acceptable under the pretense of Christian liberty (cf. v. 6).

The doctrine of Balaam, which is still being propagated in churches today, is the teaching that future blessings and rewards have been set aside for every Christian, solely based on Christ's finished work on Calvary and the Christian's positional standing "in Christ". Thus, all Christians— regardless of their conduct during the present time - will receive crowns and positions of power and authority with Christ in the [millennial] kingdom.

However, the teaching throughout the Word of God is to the contrary. The Israelites did not sin with immunity, and neither can Christians. Sin in the camp of Israel resulted in the Israelites being overthrown in the wilderness and it will be no different for Christians.

STIRRING EXHORTATION (Revelation 2:16)

"Repent; or else I will come unto thee quickly, and will fight against them with the sword of my mouth"

If the erring believers would not judge themselves and repent, they must anticipate God's judgment (cf. 1 Corinthians 11:31). Unwillingness to repent shows that a person is not a faithful believer. They would die by the sword proceeding from Christ's mouth. Balaam had died, ironically, by the Israelites' sword (Numbers 31:8).

This judgment would be by the unyielding standard of God's revealed Word that clearly condemns such behavior.

ENDURING PROMISE (Revelation 2:17)

"He that hath an ear, let him hear what the Spirit saith

unto the churches; To him that overcometh will I give to eat of the hidden manna, and will give him a white stone, and in the stone a new name written, which no man knoweth saving he that receiveth it."

The "hidden manna" here is apparently a reference to the manna that sustained the Israelites in the wilderness that lay "hidden" in the holy of holies. The Christians in Pergamos did not need the food of pagan festivals, since they already had much better food.

Christians feed spiritually on Jesus Christ, the Bread of Life (John 6:48-51), who is the real Manna hidden from sight now.

Victors in contests or battles also received a white stone. Perhaps, God will elevate the overcomer to the position of ruler over the earth and will give him or her a new name, as He did Joseph (cf. Genesis 41:39-45). The name on that stone is new in the sense of being different, not new in contrast to what is old. However, the name is probably that of Christ (cf. Philippians 2:9). It is unknown to others in the sense that others who are not overcomers do not possess it.

CENTRAL TRUTH

Whatever God hates in the past is still the same thing He hates even now and forever. He will not compromise His standard.

PRAYERS

1. Oh, Lord, deliver me from the seat of power and control of Satan.
2. Powers in my city, workplace, state or nations that want to overthrow my faith, be paralyzed in Jesus' name.
3. Every ruling power of Pergamos from my father's house, place of birth, place of work, and place of my faith that wants to paralyze my faith in God, die by fire, in Jesus' name.

STUDY 11

PREVAILING OVER THE SPIRITUAL TOXINS OF LAODICEA

TEXT: REVELATION 3:14-22

"And unto the angel of the church of the Laodiceans write; These things saith the Amen, the faithful and true witness, the beginning of the creation of God; I know thy works, that thou art neither cold nor hot: I would thou wert cold or hot. So then because thou art lukewarm, and neither cold nor hot, I will spue thee out of my mouth. Because thou sayest, I am rich, and increased with goods, and have need of nothing; and knowest not that thou art wretched, and miserable, and poor, and blind, and naked: I counsel thee to buy of me gold tried in the fire, that thou mayest be rich; and white raiment, that thou mayest be clothed, and that the shame of thy nakedness do not appear; and anoint thine eyes with eyesalve, that thou mayest see. As many as I love, I rebuke and chasten: be zealous therefore, and repent. Behold, I stand at the door, and knock: if any man hear my voice, and open the door, I will come in to him, and will sup with him, and he with me. To him that overcometh will I grant to sit with me in my throne,

even as I also overcame, and am set down with my Father in his throne. He that hath an ear, let him hear what the Spirit saith unto the churches."

Jesus Christ sent this letter to shake the Laodicean Christians out of their self-sufficient complacency and to exhort them to self-sacrifice for higher spiritual goals (cf. Colossians 2:1-2,4:16).

DESTINATION AND DESCRIPTION OF CHRIST (Revelation 3:14)

"And unto the angel of the church of the Laodiceans write; These things saith the Amen, the faithful and true witness, the beginning of the creation of God."

The last of the seven cities (modern Eski-hisar, "The Old Fortress") lay about 40 miles southeast of Philadelphia and 90 miles east of Ephesus. It was a wealthy town that specialized in banking, producing black woolen cloth, and health care. It had suffered a severe earthquake that had destroyed it, but its prosperous citizens had rebuilt it.

Jesus Christ called Himself the "Amen" (meaning, "So Be It"). We should probably understand this title as a testimony to His ability to produce what He predicts (cf. Isaiah 65:16). As a "Witness," His testimony to the situation in Laodicea was trustworthy.

The Laodiceans had a reputation for saying and doing whatever was necessary to preserve their own wellbeing. In contrast, Jesus spoke the truth. The "Beginning (Origin) of God's creation" sets forth His authority to pass judgment. The Laodiceans were creative, but Jesus alone was the Creator (cf. John 1:3; Colossians 1:16).

DAMNING REBUKE (Revelation 3:15-17)

"I know thy works, that thou art neither cold nor hot: I would thou wert cold or hot. So then because thou art lukewarm, and neither cold nor hot, I will spue thee out of my mouth. Because thou sayest, I am rich, and increased with goods, and have need of nothing; and knowest not that thou art wretched, and miserable, and poor, and blind, and naked."

This church received no commendation, a fact that makes this letter unique compared to the other six. The deeds of the Laodicean Christians manifested their heart attitude; they were neither cold nor hot in their love for God, just lukewarm.

Beverages are better served either cold or hot. Similarly, the Lord would rather that His people be cold or hot in their love for Him, not apathetic.

The Laodiceans enjoyed material prosperity (v. 17) that led them to a false sense of security and independence. Spiritually, they had great needs (cf. Romans 7:24).

This self-sufficient attitude is a constant danger when Christians live lives of ease and enjoy plenty.

INSTRUCTIVE EXHORTATION (Revelation 3:18-19)

"I counsel thee to buy of me gold tried in the fire, that thou mayest be rich; and white raiment, that thou mayest be clothed, and that the shame of thy nakedness do not appear; and anoint thine eyes with eyesalve, that thou mayest see."

Since the Laodiceans considered themselves to be rich but were spiritually poor, Jesus urged them to "buy," implying self-sacrifice, the things they really needed (cf. Isaiah 55:1). Instead of real gold, they should buy "gold refined by fire," namely, pure spiritual riches (cf. Psalm 66:10; Proverbs 17:3; Zechariah 13:9; Luke 12:21; 1 Tim. 6:18; James 1:3; 2:5; 1 Peter 1:7; 4:12). Instead of the black garments that were popular in Laodicea, they should buy "white garments" that symbolize righteous conduct (19:8). Instead of the eye salve that the Laodiceans produced and sold, they should purchase spiritual "eye salve," a reference to the Word of God that enables us to see life realistically (cf. John 9:6; 1 John 2:20, 27).

Moreover, the Lord reminded the Laodiceans that His rebukes are driven by love (cf. Proverbs 3:11-12). They should, therefore, be zealous ("hot," vv. 15, 16) and repent (i.e., repent with zeal). The only way cold people can become hot in their love for the Lord is to repent (i.e., change their minds).

BENEVOLENT PROMISE (Revelation 3:20-22)

"Behold, I stand at the door, and knock: if any man hear my voice, and open the door, I will come in to him, and will sup with him, and he with me. To him that overcometh will I grant to sit with me in my throne, even as I also overcame, and am set down with my Father in his throne. He that hath an ear, let him hear what the Spirit saith unto the churches."

Jesus Christ desires intimate fellowship with all people (cf. Mark 10:45; Luke 19:10; John 10:10; 1 Timothy 4:10). The privilege of reigning with Christ will be the portion of the overcomer (cf. Matt. 19:28; Luke 22:29-30; 1 Cor. 6:2-3; 2 Tim. 2:12).

Many Revelation students have compared the Laodicean church to the church as it exists in the world today. Christendom (all professing Christians) appears wealthy and powerful, but it lacks life and love for Jesus Christ. Sadly, this is also true to a lesser degree in the body of Christ.

CENTRAL TRUTH

Material wealth or riches, if not well handled, could constitute a major threat to the spiritual growth of believers and become a toxin that will choke the life of God from them. Jesus spoke of this in the parable of the sower that through the deceitfulness of riches, a man can lose his soul (Matthew 13:22).

PRAYERS:

1. Oh Lord, deliver me from false spirituality.
2. Oh, Lord, make me alive to you by your Spirit.
3. Oh Lord, deliver me from the deceit of materialism and love of the world.

STUDY 12

THE SACRIFICE OF SELF (2)

TEXTS: Romans 12:1-2; Galatians 2:20; Philippians 3:7-11; 2 Corinthians 8:1-7; 9:6-15, 1 Kings 17:8-16; 2 Samuel 6:9-12

A sacrifice is that which we give to the Lord painfully and without a bargain. In a sacrifice, the focus is not what comes to us but what goes out of us to meet definite needs. It is measured, not by what we give, but what is left after giving.

Sacrifice of self involves use of our life, body, time, talents, money, property, contacts, and connections for the purpose of God. In the service of God, it is not expected that one charge for his endowments, even though one could be appreciated or rewarded. But the real reward is that which ultimately comes from God for being faithful to His cause. The Lord never owes any man.

Understanding this will strengthen us not to look back in making any kingdom-related sacrifice; for "He which soweth sparingly shall reap also sparingly; and he which soweth bountifully shall reap also bountifully" (2 Corinthians 9:6)

WHY RENDER SERVICE?

- Everything we have, including our skills, is from God – Exodus 35:30-35.
- We owe it to God who has given us life and salvation – Matthew 18:21-35
- Whatever service we render is the seed that we are sowing – 2 Corinthians 9:6, Genesis 8:22.
- The world is full of needy people.
- We become co-laborers with God, which is a privilege – 2 Corinthians 6:1.
- As we labor for God, He labors for us.
- The kingdom of God is very near; all hands need to be on deck.
- The harvest is fully ripe, and workers are needed.
- The Great Commission is a command of the Lord and not a suggestion. - Matthew 28:18-20
- There is an eternal reward for faithful service.
- Service (sacrifice) is a show of righteousness – 2 Corinthians 9:9

HOW TO RENDER SERVICE – Ephesians 6:5-8, Colossians 3:23

- Work with all your heart – Colossians 3:23
- Serve as though you are working for the Lord Jesus
- Serve with obedience to your Overseer – Ephesians 6v5
- Don't work with eye service. There is an unseen eye that weighs every work and attitude.
- Don't work to gain human approval.
- Serve cheerfully. God loves cheerful givers. – 2 Corinthians 9:7-8
- Remember that God is a rewarder.
- Be faithful and trustworthy – Luke 12:42-44
- Be fair and just, especially as a supervisor – Colossians 4:1, Job 31:13-15
- Work honestly – Leviticus 19:35-36
- Shun envy, malice, competition and comparison.

SCRIPTURAL EXAMPLES OF SERVICE

Consecration or self-sacrifice will manifest itself in service. Self-sacrifice must first be in place before anyone can serve the Lord effectively. Speaking of the churches of Macedonia, for example, Paul said, they "first gave their own selves to the Lord, and unto us by the will of God" (2 Corinthians 8:5).

Other Scriptural examples of people who rendered acceptable service include:

1. Obed-Edom - 2 Samuel 6:9-12

When no one else was willing to care for the ark of God but rather saw it as an instrument of death, Obed-Edom undertook to bring it into his house and take care of it. That was a great sacrifice. "And the Lord blessed Obededom, and all his household." (2 Samuel 6:11)

Notice that immediately David realized that it was a privilege to care for the things of God, he went and took the ark from the house of Obed-Edom with joy.

2. The widow of Zarephath – 1 Kings 17:8-16

Service to the Lord is also in caring for servants of the Lord. The widow giving her last meal to a man of God was a great sacrifice and service to the Lord. And the Lord blessed her in return. "She, and he, and her house, did eat many days. And the barrel of meal wasted not, neither did the cruse of oil fail, according to the word of the Lord, which he spake by Elijah." (1 Kings 17:15-16)

3. The Corinthian Church – 2 Corinthians 9:6-15

Service to the Lord also involves ministering to the needs of the saints. Ministering to the needs of saints not only blesses and encourages them but also releases a harvest of thanksgiving unto God.

SERVICE IN THE HOUSE OF GOD

There are various ways in which you can render service in the house of God.

- You can make your gifts and talents available to the house of God. These include skill in playing musical instruments, singing, decorating etc.
- You can make professional service available to the Lord. For example, a lawyer can render legal services and a doctor can render medical services. A florist can help beautify the church with flowers etc.
- You can help in ushering or social works to welcome people to church.
- You can teach in the Sunday school or new believers class.
- You can help take care of the children.
- You can help keep the church clean and tidy.

- You can be useful in visitation to church members.
- You can serve in the prayer team.
- You can support the media outreaches of the church.
- You can provide your house for fellowship meetings or make your car available for an emergency or provide just one gallon of fuel from your tank in times of scarcity.
- You can make yourself available to paste posters for a major church program or to just give out a church handbill to a neighbor.

What can you do for God now in his house without looking for a reward from the church?

The avenues for service in the house of God are endless. You can meet your pastor and discuss with him how you can be of the best service in your local assembly.

CONCLUSION

Everyone can be useful in the house of God. You don't need a title, nor do you have to be a leader or worker in the house of God to serve. All you need is love for God. Submit yourself to God for service, training and operations, and see how God will bless you.

Everyone has something to contribute. Everyone has

something to give. God asked Moses "What do you have in your hand?" it was a shepherd's rod. But when he laid it in consecration before the LORD, it became an instrument of signs and wonders. Don't despise anything God has put in your hand, whether big or small. It can feed a multitude when you put it in the hands of the master. Who would believe that a little boy's lunch, in the hands of Jesus, could feed a multitude?

But God must get your attention first. Your life must be laid upon the altar of God's purposes and plans. Then and only then will your sacrifices, gifts, talents and services avail much in the house of God. There is a place for you to serve in God's house.

PRAYERS

1. Lord, deliver me from myself and the spirit of self that will destroy me.
2. Help me, Lord, to give myself away to you in reckless abandon.
3. Father, help me to plunge myself into the service of your kingdom and humanity.

STUDY 13

DELIVERANCE FROM SELF INIQUITY

TEXT: Psalm 18:20-24

> *"The Lord rewarded me according to my righteousness; according to the cleanness of my hands hath, He recompensed me. For I have kept the ways of the Lord and have not wickedly departed from my God. For all His judgments were before me, and I did not put away His statutes from me. I was also upright before Him, and I kept myself from mine iniquity. Therefore hath the Lord recompensed me according to my righteousness, according to the cleanness of my hands in His eyesight."*

It is indeed true that every one of us has his or her own special iniquities that we enjoy! Before you exonerate yourself and declare your holiness and self-righteousness, let the word of God beam its searchlight unto every hidden area of your life.

No man can declare his own righteousness without the master declaring him righteous! Proverbs 20:6 queries,

"Most men will proclaim everyone his own goodness: but a faithful man who can find?" Also, Job 35:2 asks, " Thinkest thou this to be right, that thou saidst, My righteousness is more than God's?"

When we stand before the HOLINESS of God, then we will know how unclean we are and then we shall declare like Prophet Isaiah, "Woe is me! for I am undone; because I am a man of unclean lips, and I dwell in the midst of a people of unclean lips: for mine eyes have seen the King, the Lord of hosts." (Isaiah 6:5).

It's amazing to see believers claim they have no self-iniquities when King David, described as man after God's heart, cried out to God to deliver him from his own iniquities! It's also amazing to know that God even declares the elements as not being clean and pure in his eyes; how much more mortal men!

Job 25:4-6 declares, " How then can man be justified with God? or how can he be clean that is born of a woman? Behold even to the moon, and it shineth not; yea, the stars are not pure in his sight. How much less man, that is a worm? and the son of man, which is a worm?"

Most times, we are guilty of the errors of Job when we multiply words against God because of our troubles and calamities! When we take personal stock of our lives, and wonder why we don't I have a breakthrough yet, we begin to think we can query God with our supposed righteousness. We ask, "Why am I not married yet?",

"Why am I not prosperous yet?", "why is my prosperity not appearing?" – "After all, I have done no iniquities; I have not killed, fornicated, committed adultery…"

Here are the answers for you in the scriptures:

> **Job 33:8-12:** *"Surely thou hast spoken in mine hearing, and I have heard the voice of thy words, saying, I am clean without transgression, I am innocent; neither is there iniquity in me. Behold, He findeth occasions against me, He counteth me for his enemy, He putteth my feet in the stocks, he marketh all my paths. Behold, in this thou art not just: I will answer thee, that God is greater than man."*

Beloved, God is greater than man! He is the only one who can acquit man from iniquity. He is the only one who can justify and declare a man righteous! We must first come to Him with our own iniquities.

WHAT ARE SELF-INIQUITIES?

Self-iniquities are the sins that are so easy for you and I to commit consciously or unconsciously. The scriptures call them "easily besetting sins!" Hebrews 12:1 says, "Wherefore seeing we also are compassed about with so great a cloud of witnesses, let us lay aside every weight, and the sin which doth so easily beset us, and let us run with patience the race that is set before us."

Self-iniquities include:

1. Malice. Some people can keep malice for years. This is one of the sins that people don't consider a big deal and feel justified to do them because they think others have wronged them and they deserve anger and judgment.

2. Anger. This iniquity is easy for some and some don't have any problems with this.

3. Lies. Some people can lie so easily, so much that when they open their mouth and say: "Good morning," one may have to open the windows to check if it's indeed morning time before responding!

4. Exaggeration. Someone once said, I saw a dog that is as big and tall as a cow or an elephant! Really? Truth is, there is no dog on earth like that! But in the quest to impress their hearers, some people stretch the truth and overstretch it! This also is an easily besetting sin! In fact, we have a lot of "pulpit exaggerators!

5. Love of money. Some will do anything for money or to improve their financial wellbeing! They don't mind diverting, looting, stealing, embezzling, cutting corners, forging documents, robbing or killing to get money.

Sometimes one wonders whether some so-called believers still have a conscience, when one sees their desperation for money or how they delay or divert other people's wages. Yet God's word says in Leviticus 19:13, " Thou salt not defraud thy neighbour, neither rob him : the wages of him that is hired shall not abide with thee all night until the morning."

6. Lust/sexual immorality. To some, this is a big deal but to others, it is not! This is because some believe that men and women should be involved or indulge in this as their passions stir them. According to them, if God doesn't want us to do this, why create the organs? Why give the passions?

But the word of God says clearly that our bodies are the temples of God and should not be destroyed by fornication or adultery! Hebrews 13:4 says, "Marriage is honorable in all, and the bed undefiled: but whoremongers and adulterers God will judge." We must not allow our passion to determine our direction! However, sometimes this iniquity doesn't go away easily except by prayers, fasting and SEPARATION from the objects of temptation.

7. Cursing. Some people can curse out anyone with all kinds of vulgarity! But the Scripture instructs in Colossians 3:8, "But now ye also put off all these; anger, wrath, malice, blasphemy, filthy communication out of your mouth."

8. Drinking alcohol and smoking. My friend once met a pastor, who, after coming out of a ministers' conference, brought out a cigarette, lighted it and started smoking! My friend asked him, "Sir, why are you smoking? Are you not a minister?" He replied, "Oh! That is my addiction! I am praying about it!"

Truly, anything you can't do away with is an addiction! And it is time to be addicted to Jesus, The word, and prayers. Do away with alcohol and smoking that can embarrass you. Proverbs 23:29-30 says, " Who hath woe? who hath sorrow? who hath contentions? who hath babbling? who hath wounds without cause? who hath redness of eyes? T hey that tarry long at the wine; they that go to seek mixed wine."

9. Flattery: When you say things, you don't mean; or when you give praise and eulogy that are not sincere, that is flattery. Job 17:5 says, "He that speaketh flattery to his friends, even the eyes of his children shall fail." Job said that the use of flattery can make God take a man away. Yet, this is one of our self-iniquities that we indulge in. One of the criteria for triumphant saints in Revelation is that "there is no guile found in their mouth." (Revelation 14:1-4).

10. Inordinate fleshly desires. There are people who cannot deny their flesh of any craving, even if such is against God's word. Sometimes, as a believer, you see things that your flesh wants but you must learn to deny your eyes, mouth and flesh from what God does not want for you.

This was what destroyed heir apparent Adonijah, son of King David (see 1 Kings 2:13-25).

11. Fantasies and secret perversions. People dark fantasies which are secret iniquities, and they might not manifest until circumstances of life and situation bring them out.

Most times, God will not give you your fantasies because they are those things that might seek to destroy you. You must deal with this iniquity by all means. King Solomon was ruined by this little fantasies which he called little foxes that destroy the vines (Song 2:15). Whatever he desired, he did not restraint himself from it and he saw that that was also vanity (Ecclesiastes 2:2-10).

STEPS TO DELIVERANCE FROM SELF-INIQUITIES

In Psalm 32:5, the Psalmist says, "I acknowledged my sin unto Thee, and mine iniquity have I not hid. I said, I will confess my transgressions unto the Lord; and Thou forgavest the iniquity of my sin."

- Identify and acknowledge your sin
- Do not give excuses; do not justify your sins.
- Find the root cause of this sin and identify its entrance!
- Disconnect from everything and anyone that brings forth the sin.
- Seek counsel and therapy, if necessary.

- Seek personal deliverance and deliverance from higher anointed men of God.
- Keep purging yourself and keep yourself from idols!

PRAYERS

1. My Father, deliver me from every self-iniquity that is easy for me to commit.
2. Every secret iniquity that will not allow me to see your face or glory in my life, my Father, knock it out and pour it out of my life in Jesus' name.
3. Oh Lord, take the dross away from my life and I shall be a vessel for the finer. (Proverbs 25 :4-5)

STUDY 14

SPIRITUAL DETOXIFICATION THROUGH FASTING

TEXTS: Matthew 9:29, Psalm 35:13, 1 Corinthians 7:5

Fasting is the denial of the flesh from all kind of pleasures, be it food, water, sex, T.V, words, association, or all kinds self-seeking and flesh-pleasing desires, in other to seek the face of God for healing, deliverance, transformation, or revelation (Isaiah 58:6-11).

WHY DO WE FAST?

1. We fast to humble ourselves in order to seek the face of God. - Psalm35:13
2. We fast to seek deliverance – 1 Samuel 7:7-10, Psalm 69:10-18
3. We fast to seek transformation - Ezra 8:21-23
4. We fast to seek forgiveness- 1 Kings 21:27-29

5. We fast to seek revival - Psalm 63:1-8
6. We fast to see the power of God and the directions of the Holy Spirit. Acts 13:1-2
7. We fast to see growth – Acts 13:2
8. We fast to break the hold of sins, iniquity and addictions - Isaiah 58:6.

13 BENEFITS AND BLESSINGS OF FASTING

1. Fasting helps your spirit to be humble.
2. Fasting helps you to be spiritually sensitive to the voice of God.
3. Fasting breaks the yokes of pride in your life.
4. Fasting helps you see things and life in a new light.
5. Fasting destroys your anxiety and worries.
6. Fasting helps you to believe the impossible is possible.
7. Fasting releases the power and authority of God in your heart and through your mouth.
8. Fasting helps you speak power and ministers in power.
9. Fasting releases fresh anointing upon your life and ministration.
10. Fasting clears your spiritual airways and beat down the powers of darkness.

11. Fasting makes your enemies and situations submit to you.

12. Fasting helps your spirit to quickly conjugate with the spirit of the Lord; therefore, you become one with the Lord.

13. Fasting helps clear toxins and sicknesses from your physical body and you become healthier, physically, mentally, and sexually.

DANGERS OF FASTING WITHOUT PRAYERS, THE WORD AND ACCOUNTABILITY

I have discovered how powerful fasting is in my own life and as I have also studied the life of a lot of great men and women of God who are giving to prayers and fasting. I have seen the blessings and the dangers of fasting without carefulness, studying of the word, indwelling, living and been controlled by the word, especially after a long fasting.

After a long fasting, these are the dangers you are exposed to:

- Pride immediately after the fast. You will feel so intoxicated with power so much that if you do not have the word in you, you will start speaking arrogantly to everyone and anyone. In fact, you will want to curse and kill anyone that appears to be rude or insulting to you.

- Sexual temptations after a long fast. You see, fasting is good spiritually to your soul and physically to your body. After a long fast, your male and female sex hormones are clean and are now aggressively active and you are ready to strike, or when you strike, you become more passionate and energetic. If there is no word and control in you by the Holy Ghost, you will want to indulge constantly in sexual activities with anyone who makes himself or herself available to you. This is the reasons most prophetic people and ministers who love to fast a long time find themselves prone to this sin. You must control yourself with the word of God that says: "Ye shall be holy: for I the Lord your God am holy." (Leviticus 19:2)

There are some anointed, prophetic people who do not control themselves by the Spirit of Holiness but always observe that after they have committed fornication or adultery, they feel more anointed and see more miracles; but it is the deception of the devil to damn their souls to destruction. Long fasting without the word, prayers, the Spirit of holiness and accountability always leads to sexual promiscuity.

- Fasting releases an anointing and glory that makes you attractive to the good, the bad and the ugly. Songs of Solomon 1:3 says, "'Because of the savor of thy good ointments thy name is as ointment poured forth, therefore, do the virgins love thee."

- Here is another danger of long fasting without prayer, the word, and accountability. After a long fasting, there is a fresh oil that is released upon your head and life (Psalm 92:10). There is a fresh glory that makes you attractive and glowing. You become attractive and attracted to all kinds of good people and bad people. The king's daughters begin to like you (Psalms 45:7-12). The nobles, politicians, intellectuals, educated, non-educated, crooks and criminals will desire you, especially when you begin to demonstrate power, authority, and anointing. Some of the women will just want to appreciate you with their body, not because they mean evil but because some will feel it is their way of appreciating the glory and anointing upon you. If you are not spirit-filled, worded and accountable, you will begin to misbehave.

- Invasion of strange spirits. Long fasting without prayers, the word and accountability can lead to the invasion and subtle penetrations of wrong spirits that will minister extra-biblical teachings, doctrines, and seductions of the devils to you. (Galatians 1:6-9). Many great monks, bishops, cardinals, and prophets who are seeking mysticisms of the spirit instead of pursuing and seeking Christ have been seduced by wrong spirits into certain delusions and apparitions of false spirits or angels who are giving them revelations from the pit of hell. This is the reason you must be accountable after your fast and special revelations to submit to fellow spiritual and mature men of God, who can judge your visions, revelations, and experiences by the Spirit of God in them.

- Fame and Prosperity. Luke 4:1-2, 14 says, "And Jesus being full of the Holy Ghost returned from Jordan, and was led by the Spirit into the wilderness, Being forty days tempted of the devil. And in those days he did eat nothing… And Jesus returned in the power of the Spirit into Galilee: and there went out a fame of him through all the region round about."

After a long period of fasting in the life of Jesus, fame and prosperity appeared. Kings and nobles sought for him. This same is true for a lot of believers and ministers of the gospel. After a long and continuous period of fasting, suddenly, prosperity, money and fame begin to appear. However, unlike Jesus, many of them are not able to handle and manage the danger of this new level. When there come money, fame and prosperity, if we don't control ourselves by constant prayers, the word and accountability, this can us begin to slip off into iniquity. We must engage in fasting but we must also be accountable and abide in the Spirit.

"If we live in the Spirit, let us also walk in the Spirit' (Galatians 5:25)

HOW TO FAST

- Fast because you loved the Lord.
- Fast because you want to see His face.
- Fast by the leading of the Holy Spirit.
- Fast periodically.
- Be medically fit to fast.
- Do not fast for competition.
- Fast to stay healthy.
- Fast for soul cleansing.
- Do not fast for boasting an arrogance.
- Be accountable after your fast.

PRAYERS

1. Father Lord, guide me by your Spirit in my fasting and praying.
2. Lord, empower me to fast and pray till your will is done in my life.
3. Lord, keep me victorious over the temptations associated with fasting.

STUDY 15

ANGELIC FOOD

TEXTS: PSALMS 78:24-24; PSALM 103:20-22.

Man is a spirit being. He was made from the dust of the earth. His flesh or body is earthly or dusty. His soul or spirit was from the breath of God or the spirit of God. So, his soul and spirit are heavenly and angelic. Jesus said, "a spirit hath not flesh and bones" (Luke 24:39)

God breathed upon man and he became a living soul or spirit. "And the LORD God formed man of the dust of the ground, and breathed into his nostrils the breath of life; and man became a living soul." (Genesis 2:7)

Man needs food to sustain his body, health, and growth. It takes sand or dust to feed dust and spirit to feed the spirit. Man's food to sustain his earthly body is grown from the earth. Your fruits, vegetables, rice, beans, yam, flour and others come out of the ground. The ground needs the ground to survive; earth needs earth to thrive; and dust needs dust to survive and grow.

For the spirit of man to also survive and grow, it needs

spirit foods. If we feed our body and don't feed our spirit, our body will grow, but our spirit will die. It takes the spirit to feed the spirit.

FOOD OF THE SPIRIT

Manna is the food of the spirit. Manna is the food of the angels. Manna is the word of God. Deuteronomy 8:3 says, "And He humbled thee, and suffered thee to hunger, and fed thee with manna, which thou knewest not, neither did thy fathers know; that He might make thee know that man doth not live by bread only, but by every word that proceedeth out of the mouth of the LORD doth man live.'

Hebrews 1:7 also says, "And of the angels he saith, Who maketh his angels spirits, and his ministers a flame of fire." So, if you must excel in strength, which is Ghibor Ghibor in Hebrew (meaning excelling in strength (Psalm 103: 20-22), you must eat angels' food. When you eat angels' food, your spiritual strength, wisdom, sanctification, holiness, power, and joy will increase.

Psalms 78:24-25 says, "And had rained down manna upon them to eat, and had given them of the corn of heaven. Man did eat angels' food: he sent them meat to the full."

Manna is the cornbread of heaven. We must eat the word of God daily, if we must grow and increase in strength (Joshua 1:8)

BLESSINGS OF EATING THE WORD OF GOD

Psalm 19:7-12 reveals, ""The law of the LORD is perfect, converting the soul: the testimony of the LORD is sure, making wise the simple. The statutes of the LORD are right, rejoicing the heart: the commandment of the LORD is pure, enlightening the eyes. The fear of the LORD is clean, enduring forever: the judgments of the LORD are true and righteous altogether. More to be desired are they than gold, yea, than much fine gold: sweeter also than honey and the honeycomb. Moreover by them is thy servant warned: and in keeping of them there is great reward. Who can understand his errors? cleanse thou me from secret faults.

Keep back thy servant also from presumptuous sins; let them not have dominion over me: then shall I be upright, and I shall be innocent from the great transgression. Let the words of my mouth, and the meditation of my heart, be acceptable in thy sight, O LORD, my strength, and my redeemer."

From the above, the blessings of eating the word of God (or angels' food) are:

- The word converts the soul.
- The word is sure and never fails; it makes you never to fail.
- The word makes you wise. 2 Timothy 3:15

- The world rejoices and gladdens your heart.
- The word makes you pure. Psalm 12:6
- The word opens your eyes to see divine mysteries and revelations. Psalm 119:18
- The word of the Lord endures forever and makes you abide in Him forever. Psalm 19: 9a
- The word of God is righteous, and it makes you righteous in Him. Psalm 19:9
- The word of God is pure, has gold and it brings prosperity. Psalm 119:14
- The word of God warns you and keeps you from iniquity. Psalm19:11
- The word of God produces faith.
- The word of God sets free.- John 8:32
- The word of God produces growth .1 Peter 2:2
- The word of God produces healing. Proverbs 4:20-22
- The word of God strengthens you to do the work of God. 2 Timothy 3:16-17.

PRAYERS

1. Father Lord, guide me by your Spirit in my fasting and praying.
2. Lord, empower me to fast and pray till your will is done in my life.
3. Lord, keep me victorious over the temptations associated with fasting.

STUDY 16

THE RECHABITES:DETOXIFYING FROM THE POWER OF ALCOHOL

TEXTS: JEREMIAH 35:1-2, PROVERBS 23:29-35

> *"The word which came unto Jeremiah from the LORD in the days of Jehoiakim the son of Josiah king of Judah, saying, Go unto the house of the Rechabites, and speak unto them, and bring them into the house of the LORD, into one of the chambers, and give them wine to drink." (Jeremiah 35:1-2)*

Caron Pennsylvania, a center for alcohol abuse and recovery, provides the following enlightening insights on alcohol:

Alcohol (also known as ethanol or ethyl alcohol) is a psychoactive drug that acts as a central nervous system depressant. Alcohol interferes with communication between nerve cells and all other cells and affects various centers in the brain. Even moderate alcohol consumption causes immediate effects, such as lowered inhibitions, increased relaxation and dulled senses." As alcohol consumption (and blood alcohol) increases, users may experience:

- heightened emotional responses (including anger and aggression)
- lack of coordination
- poor balance
- slurred speech
- dizziness
- disturbed sleep
- nausea and vomiting

Alcohol affects the body in stages, causing various states of being, including:

- relaxation
- euphoria
- excitement
- confusion
- stupor

Extreme alcohol consumption can cause memory loss (blackouts), complete loss of coordination and alcohol poisoning. In some cases, alcohol overdose can be fatal.

Other short-term effects of alcohol include harm to the body's tissues:

- **Stomach:** Alcohol irritates the stomach and intestine lining and increases stomach acid secretion. This causes vomiting.
- **Skin:** Alcohol increases blood flow to the skin, causing users to sweat and appear flushed.
- **Muscles:** Alcohol and reduces blood flow to the muscles, causing muscle aches (most notably felt as the alcohol leaves the system.) This effect is often called a hangover.

The severity of the effects of alcohol is dependent on a variety of factors, including the weight, age and sex of the individual consuming the alcohol and how much was eaten before and during consumption. Alcohol is eventually metabolized and eliminated from the system at a rate of 13 to 18 mg per hour.

LONG-TERM EFFECTS OF ALCOHOL ABUSE

Excessive use can lead to abuse and dependence, both of which may ultimately require treatment. Individuals who abuse alcohol may develop physical symptoms upon abrupt discontinuation or drastic reduction of alcohol consumption. As with any drug addiction, physical dependence and withdrawal symptoms from alcohol will develop in anyone who has regularly been drinking heavily for an extended period of time if and when intake is suddenly curtailed.

SPIRITUAL DANGERS OF ALCOHOLISM

It is important to note that aside from the health hazards posed by alcohol consumption, as explained by the Caron center above, alcohol also has so much power and effect on man's spirit. It was apparently in consideration of this that the grandfather of the Rechabites in Jeremiah 35, made his children and grandchildren to enter into a covenant of not touching wine or alcoholic drink all the days of their lives.

Now, it happened that in order to illustrate a powerful spiritual truth to the Israelites, God told Jeremiah, a renowned prophet - tested and approved by God and men - to bring the Rechabites into the temple and offer them wine to drink. But the Rechabites refused, saying that their father had made them to promise him not to touch alcohol or strong wine, and they had never touched any alcohol or strong drinks.

Regarding the effects of alcohol on the spirit of man, Proverbs 23:29-35 says,

"'Who hath woe? Who hath sorrow?
Who hath contentions?
Who hath babbling? who hath wounds without cause?
Who hath redness of eyes?
They that tarry long at the wine;
they that go to seek mixed wine.
Look not thou upon the wine when it is red,
when it giveth his colour in the cup,
when it moveth itself aright.
At the last, it biteth like a serpent,
and stingeth like an adder.
Thine eyes shall behold strange women,
and thine heart shall utter perverse things.
Yea, thou salt be as he that lieth down in the midst of the sea,
or as he that lieth upon the top of a mast.
They have stricken me, salt thou say, and I was not sick;
they have beaten me, and I felt it not:
when shall I awake? I will seek it yet again.'"

Strong drinks have so much effect on a man's spirit, soul and body that it begins to make him do the following:

1. He becomes disorganized and disoriented.
2. He begins to blab nonsense and can let out dark secrets that can destroy his home, marriage, business and career.
3. He has redness of eyes.
4. He is incoherent and abusive to his spouse, children, staff, or colleagues.
5. It makes him lose his honor and position.
6. He loses balance
7. He can pee on himself and staff vomiting.
8. He can lie on the road or fall by the wayside, thinking he is on his bed.

No wonder the Scripture says that strong drinks and alcohol should be given to him that is ready to perish. So, except you are ready to perish, you must not indulge in strong drinks and alcohol. Proverbs 31:5-6 reveals, "'Give strong drink unto him that is ready to perish, and wine unto those that be of heavy hearts.

Let him drink, and forget his poverty, and remember his misery no more."

So, we have the proof that, scripturally speaking, strong wine and alcohol are for those who are ready to perish. Men who will serve God and do well in life for themselves and their family, society, ministry and business cannot indulge in alcoholism. If the Rechabites could reject wine, even from a prophet, you can also reject strong drinks from your friends, colleagues, or other sources.

Your love for God and your future and destiny will keep you from strong drinks like the Rechabites. Your destiny and future are very important. Besides, you want to consider your finances because strong drinks lead people into poverty. Proverbs 31: 4-7 warns,

"It is not for kings, O Lemuel, it is not for kings to drink wine;
nor for princes strong drink:
Lest they drink, and forget the law,
and pervert the judgment of any of the afflicted.
Give strong drink unto him that is ready to perish,
and wine unto those that be of heavy hearts.
Let him drink, and forget his poverty,
and remember his misery no more.'

These verses further reveal that:

- When you take too much of strong drinks, you will forget the laws of God.

- When you take strong drinks, you will pervert justice.
- When you take strong drinks and too much, you might not be able to reach your potential and leadership because, strong drinks are not meant for kings – that is, leaders, pastors, ministers or CEOs
- Strong drinks rob you of your mental capacities.
- Strong drinks have led to ruins of marriages, lives, careers and greatness.

PROCESS OF DETOXIFICATION

"If a man therefore purge himself from these, he shall be a vessel unto honor, sanctified, and meet for the master's use, and prepared unto every good work." 2 Timothy 2:21

Beloved, the Scripture is clear that if you are going to be used by God, you must purge (detoxify) yourself from anything and anyone that may corrupt or contaminate your soul. We are vessels unto honor and therefore, we cannot indulge in anything that will contaminate our body, soul or spirit, or that has any appearance of evil.

How do we detoxify from strong drinks?

- Acknowledge it if you are indulging in it.
- Ask God to forgive you and purge you.

- Be accountable to a group, a leader or an individual that helps you.
- Seek deliverance.
- Avoid associations and places that will spark up this desire in you.
- Learn to say no like the Rechabites, no matter who is offering you the drink.
- Constantly be accountable and responsible to yourself.

PRAYERS

1. My father, deliver me from anything that I love that can destroy my life and future.
2. Father save me from any addictions or inherited devils of my father's house.
3. I purge myself by the blood of Jesus from anything that defiles and corrupts my spirit.

STUDY 17

WHAT DID JESUS TRULY PROMISE US?

Text: 1 John 2:25

> *"And this is the promise that he hath promised us, even eternal life."*

> *The greatest promise from God to mankind is ETERNAL LIFE. Jesus did not promise prosperity, although it's in the package! The main course is "eternal life", nothing more or less! Breakthrough, healing, deliverance, success and other blessings are all in the package but the primary blessing is life eternal (Matthew 6:33).*

Let's go for the main course and leave the dessert!

The primary purpose of Jesus' coming into the world is clearly stated in Matthew 1:21 "And she shall bring forth a son, and thou shalt call his name Jesus: for he shall save his people from their sins."

Contrary to the gospels that we preach today, especially

the gospels of prosperity, breakthroughs and other sweet delicacies of the consumer gospel, Jesus never emphasized any of such things, although it's in the package.

The main course of the gospel is eternity. That is the bread, the substance and the life of the gospel. Prosperity and others are icings on the cake. The icing can be detrimental to your health if you eat too much of it. You need the bread! The body, the main course. Jesus said, "I am the living bread which came down from heaven: if any man eat of this bread, he shall live forever: and the bread that I will give is my flesh, which I will give for the life of the world." (John 6:51)

SOURCE OF ETERNAL LIFE

Eternal life comes from receiving Jesus into our lives. John 17:3 says, "And this is life eternal, that they might know thee the only true God, and Jesus Christ, whom thou hast sent". Jesus is the eternal life. Eternal life is in Him. To have Him and know Him is to have eternal life. 1 John 5:20 explains, "And we know that the Son of God is come, and hath given us an understanding, that we may know Him that is true, and we are in Him that is true, even in His Son Jesus Christ. This is the true God, and eternal life."

Essentially, the Bible says:

- The Son came from God.

- The Son came to give us understanding.
- We are in Him.
- We know Him.
- The true God is Christ.
- Christ is the eternal life.
- To have Christ is to have eternal and daily walk-in eternal life and towards eternity.

IS PROSPERITY A SIN?

3 John 2 says, "Beloved, I wish above all things that thou mayest prosper and be in health, even as thy soul prospereth."

Many wonder why we lay so much emphasis on the spiritual and eternal. They wonder, Does God want me to proper or does He prefer me to live in poverty to the glory of his name?

First and foremost, there is nothing glorifying to God in poverty, though God might be glorified through your poverty.

The best poverty is the poverty of the soul and spirit. To be poor in the spirit is to be rich in seeking God and having more of God. Matthew 5:3 says, "Blessed are the poor in spirit: for theirs is the kingdom of heaven."

God wants to prosper us as Christians. As a matter of fact, the Bible says God has pleasure in the prosperity of his servant. "Let them shout for joy, and be glad, that favour My righteous cause: yea, let them say continually, Let the Lord be magnified, which hath pleasure in the prosperity of His servant. (Psalm 35:27)

God has pleasure in your prosperity. But before the prosperity of the pocket, bank accounts, houses, etc., God has pleasure in the prosperity of the soul

To be rich in the pocket but poor in the soul is dangerous to mankind. Those who are not rich in the spirit but rich in the pocket will harm people, manipulate, cheat and set a whole nation on fire. Why? The thought of God and eternity is not in them. Psalms 10:4 says, "The wicked, through the pride of his countenance, will not seek after God: God is not in all his thoughts."

PROSPERITY ON PURPOSE

Why would God want you to prosper? There is a purpose for kingdom prosperity and there is a caution that comes with it.

1. God wants His kingdom and mission to spread through your prosperity.

Zechariah 1:17 says, "Cry yet, saying, Thus saith the Lord of hosts; My cities through prosperity shall yet be spread abroad; and the Lord shall yet comfort Zion,

and shall yet choose Jerusalem."

When you prosper, God wants you to use your prosperity to propagate the gospel of his kingdom, build His church and spread His work around the world.

2. God wants you to give to the poor.

"Blessed is he that considereth the poor: the LORD will deliver him in time of trouble. The LORD will preserve him, and keep him alive; and he shall be blessed upon the earth: and thou wilt not deliver him unto the will of his enemies.' (Psalm 41: 1-2).

Prosperity is meant for you to be a blessing to others. This does not mean that you are Jehovah El-Shaddai, who shall supply all the needs of the whole world. You bless people as you are led, not as by your feelings. Be wise here.

3. God wants you to do good to your fellow brethren in the household of faith. He wants you to lend to them without interest but with the agreement of payback when you are lending.

Galatians 6:10 says, "As we have therefore opportunity, let us do good unto all men, especially unto them who are of the household of faith."

Exodus 22:25 also says, "'If thou lend money to any of my people that is poor by thee, thou salt not be to him as an usurer, neither salt thou lay upon him usury."

4. God prospers you so you can support every righteous and good cause.

Psalm 35:27 again says, "Let them shout for joy, and be glad, that favors my righteous cause: yea, let them say continually, Let the LORD be magnified, which hath pleasure in the prosperity of his servant."

In essence, God blesses you so you can favor His righteous cause. Righteous causes are causes that that promote God's kingdom agenda, His kingdom work, project, building and anything else that blesses His kingdom.

PRAYERS

1. Dear, Lord, help me to prioritize your kingdom and eternal life more than every other blessing.
2. Father, help me to have the right understanding of prosperity, so I do not abuse it.
3. Lord, help me to use your blessings upon me to glorify your name and bless humanity.

STUDY 18

RUN TO OBTAIN

Text: 1 Corinthians 9:24-27

> *Ecclesiastes 9:11 says, "I returned and saw under the sun, that the race is not to the swift, nor the battle to the strong, neither yet bread to the wise, nor yet riches to men of understanding, nor yet favour to men of skill; but time and chance happeneth to them all."*

The Christian race is a race not for the strongest, the swiftest, the wisest, or the most skilled persons; rather, it is a race for the obedient and those who seek a reward at the end from the Father of life who has called them.

We are called to run a race in other to obtain a reward from our God. We must run the race in accordance with the rules, so we can get a reward in the end. .

This race cannot be run by your own standard and rules; it must be run according to God's rules and standard; then and only then can we OBTAIN.

RUNNING BY THE RULES

The rules for this race require certain prerequisites, and if we don't run by these conditions, we might just run in vain and cannot obtain any reward. 1 Corinthians 3:10-15 says, "According to the grace of God which is given unto me, as a wise masterbuilder, I have laid the foundation, and another buildeth thereon. But let every man take heed how he buildeth thereupon. For other foundation can no man lay than that is laid, which is Jesus Christ. Now if any man build upon this foundation gold, silver, precious stones, wood, hay, stubble; Every man's work shall be made manifest: for the day shall declare it, because it shall be revealed by fire; and the fire shall try every man's work of what sort it is. If any man's work abide which he hath built thereupon, he shall receive a reward. If any man's work shall be burned, he shall suffer loss: but he himself shall be saved; yet so as by fire."

1. Holiness - 1 Peter 1:15-16.

"Be ye holy; for I am holy"

Holiness is a number one prerequisite (condition) for this race. Satan can fake everything, but He cannot fake holiness because to be holy is to be free from all appearances of evil and evil itself. (1 Thessalonians 5:22)

2. Love out of a pure heart – Romans 12:9-10

The Christian race must be run with a genuine love for Christ and the brotherhood of Christ.

3. Faith - Hebrews 10:38

The Christian race is a race of faith. Doubt, unbelief and discouragement cannot survive this race. There are afflictions and trials along the path of this race. We need constant and consistent faith in the finished works of the grace of our Lord Jesus Christ to survive and obtain at the end of this race.

4. Patience - Hebrews 10:35-36

The Scripture says we have a need of "PATIENCE" to obtain. Without patience, we cannot survive this race and we cannot obtain the reward and the promises. Patience will make us bear the reproach of Christ, suffer the slights of men, partake of his suffering and at the end receive the crown that is laid down for us.

We cannot patiently endure if our eyes are off "Jesus." To patiently endure, we must keep our eyes and heart steadfastly on Jesus, for that is the only way we cannot see what the enemies are doing to us; that is the only way we can survive the HOSTILITIES AND TAUNTING OF MEN on this race! Hebrews 12:3

A song composer says:

"Don't lose your vision of Jesus; keep your eyes steadfast on Him; many have fallen on the way, and many are holding still on him."

5. Steadfastness - Hebrews 3:12-15

Steadfastness is not the same thing as endurance. Endurance is the ability to go through certain situations and conditions, while steadfastness is the ability to remain stable on the same track of the race; that is, not being moved to another race or another gospel.

Steadfastness is the ability to maintain and retain that which we have received from Christ; not soon shaken or driven by every wind of doctrines to another faith, profession, or confession that is not part of the "ANCIENT LANDMARKS" of the gospel which we have received from our fathers.

Paul warns us not to be removed from the grace of this race (Galatians 1:6-8). He also warns us against every wind of doctrine that might want to move us (Ephesians 4:11-15). Believers in Christ must be careful in this day and age because there are many winds of different gospels that are trying to remove us from the original gospel of the cross of Christ Jesus our Lord. These new-age gospels are watering down the potency and the message of the cross and turning the grace of God into lasciviousness.

6. Sacrifice - Romans 12:1-2

To run this race, we must be willing to sacrifice every comfort of our flesh. We must be willing to lay our flesh on the altar of His cross and fire, and die to ourselves for us to be able to run well and obtain the reward.

This race of Christ calls for sacrifice. We must be willing to sacrifice our all to get to the place of glory and reward. "Then said Jesus unto his disciples, If any man will come after me, let him deny himself, and take up his cross, and follow me.

For whosoever will save his life shall lose it: and whosoever will lose his life for my sake shall find it." (Matthew 16:24-25).

Essentially, to follow Christ, run to the end and obtain the reward, you must:

- Deny your sinful friends and forsake them
- Deny your evil company and forsake them
- Deny your occultic and demonic groups and forsake them.

7. Prayer - Luke 18:1

Prayer is the fuel for the race; prayer is the funnel through which heavenly strength and energy are supplied for the race.

Prayer is the funnel through which our spirit of the race is renewed by the Holy Ghost (Titus 3:4-5).

Charles G. Finney said of prayer:

"There is nothing in the whole Christian religion so rarely

attained as a praying heart. Without this, you are weak as weakness itself. With it, you are irresistible. If you lose your spirit of prayer, you will do nothing, or next to nothing, though you have the intellectual endowment of an angel."

Alexander Whyte said:

"The greatest and the best talent that God gives to any man or woman in this world is the talent to pray.

Mathew Skariah added:

"When we bow before God in prayer, we actually allow Him to pour himself into us immeasurably."

Prayer takes a holy resolve.

CONCLUSION

If we don't run the race with the above conditions, we cannot obtain the prize.

PRAYERS:

1. Father, help me to run the race that is set before me.
2. Father, help me not to run another man's race.
3. Father, help me to remain focus and keep a straight path for my feet.

Made in the USA
Monee, IL
07 May 2021

66859935R00079